THE EARLY
CHRISTIANS

Michael Gough

81 PHOTOGRAPHS
38 LINE DRAWINGS
AND 1 MAP

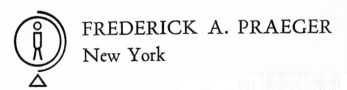

FREDERICK A. PRAEGER
New York

THIS IS VOLUME NINETEEN IN THE SERIES

Ancient Peoples and Places

GENERAL EDITOR: DR. GLYN DANIEL

BOOKS THAT MATTER   *Published in the United States of America
in 1961 by Frederick A. Praeger, Inc.
Publisher, 64 University Place
New York 3, N.Y.*

Library of Congress Catalog Card Number: 61–9981
© *Michael Gough 1961*
Printed in Great Britain by Jarrold and Sons Ltd., Norwich

CONTENTS

ILLUSTRATIONS

9

To
my mother

Foreword

Plate 1

THE FIRST fourteen verses of St John's Gospel set out the basic doctrine of the Christian religion, the doctrine of the Incarnation. This is the article of faith that unites all Christians of today with one another and with their co-religionists of the primitive Church, and which provides a continuity that is independent of place or people.

The story of the Early Christians is therefore limited only in time, and the real problem here is to decide on an acceptable definition of the word 'early'. To some it will suggest the period up to the Edict of Toleration in 313, or before 410 when Rome was sacked by the barbarians; there is, however, much to be said for the choice of the year 527 as a lower limit. It is the year of Justinian's accession, and effectively marks the end of an old era and the beginning of a new.

Before his time, although Constantinople had been in fact the sole effective capital of what remained of the Roman Empire for more than a century, the prestige and influence of Rome still left its impress on every department of the city's official life. Two Consuls, annually appointed, propped up the rickety façade of the ancient state edifice, against which the farce of an Emperor in Constantinople responsible to the Senate and People of Rome was still enacted, and in a cosmopolitan city whose predominant elements were Oriental and Greek, Latin remained the language of officialdom. Statues to the Emperors and memorials to their victories were set up in the new capital, as earlier they had been in Rome under their pagan predecessors. From 527 onwards the last tenuous links with ancient Rome were snapped one by one, and Constantinople, in the person of the Emperor, became undisputed leader of a new Empire based on the authority, under imperial safeguards, of the Christian Church.

Some five hundred years were enough to see the trans-formation of what at first appeared to be an obscure Jewish cult into the main spiritual impulse of a great Empire, and it is this period, this five hundred years, that forms the chronological background to this book; but since it is evident that the status of the Church and the fortunes of its individual members under-went a complete change with the more liberal policies intro-duced by Rome in 313, this natural break is utilized to divide the story of the Early Christians into two parts.

The subject matter of such a book as this is so wide in scope that it is perhaps inevitable that there should be some anomalies and discrepancies. Thus, in the chapter entitled 'The First Three Centuries of Christianity' very little space is devoted to the early heresies; on the other hand, they occupy a large part of the later historical chapter 'From Constantine to Justinian'. This change of emphasis is deliberate, since in the early centuries the most important factors affecting the Church were political, while later, theological discussion dominated the life of the Christian world. Again, in the chapter 'Christian Architecture before Constantine' the scantiness of material evidence leaves an opportunity for a short description of the early development of the liturgy, which is omitted in the later chapters on Christian architecture in face of the wealth of actual remains to be described.

Christian doctrine is a matter for the theologian; the men and women who in the past have applied it to their lives are a subject for historical and archaeological study; but since Christian civilization is a literate one and is documented almost from its beginnings down to our own day, the archaeological record is not so often a primary source as it is in the case of illiterate folk, or of the peoples of antiquity like the Hittites or the Etruscans, whose historical continuity has been broken once and for all. Nevertheless, the archaeological material is always of value as evidence, confirmatory or otherwise, of the reliability of the literary sources, and indispensable whenever (as so often it does for the first three centuries of the Church) it throws new light on the life, thought, art and material possessions of these early followers of Christ. The approach of this book to the subject is in the main archaeological, but the availability of a literary record is used to provide the background and a brief historical introduction to each part.

My sincere thanks are due to all those friends and colleagues who have so generously put their time and knowledge at my disposal, not only while this book was being written, but for many years before. In Great Britain I owe a special debt to Professors Sir William Calder, Stuart Piggott, and D. Talbot Rice, and to the Rev. J. H. Crehan, s.j., for their interest and stimulating criticism. I am also happy to acknowledge more than ten years of encouragement by Mr Seton Lloyd, Director of the British Institute of Archaeology at Ankara, and the facilities so freely granted to me by the Turkish General Directorate of Museums and Antiquities for my work in Asia Minor. In Italy I have greatly benefited too from the advice of Mr J. B. Ward-Perkins, the Director, and Mr M. Ballance, the Assistant Director of the British School at Rome, and from the meticulous care given by Mr Islay Lyons in producing new and arresting photographs of many monu-ments in Rome. Dr Ludwig Budde of the University of Münster has also been kind enough to allow me to publish his original photographs of the recently excavated mosaic at Misis (Mopsuestia) in the Cilician Plain.

Finally, I wish to thank Mrs W. Bryher for her sustained interest and characteristic generosity in supporting my work over a number of years, and my wife for putting her skill at my disposal in drawing so many objects and plans for insertion in the text, and for her patience in reading and criticizing the book from the first to the last word.

Introduction: The Background

To UNDERSTAND the first Christians one must first understand the broad outlines of the world into which Christianity was born. It was geographical, no less than political factors that determined the direction and rate of spread of the new religion from its original home in the Roman province of Judaea, and geography too that gave rise to such diversity in its outward expression, particularly in the field of architecture and art.

The world of the first century A.D. was a new world and an old world. The monolithic uniformity imposed by Imperial Rome on the Mediterranean litoral from the Straits of Gibraltar to the Levant was an unprecedented phenomenon, and so obscured the old order of things that it comes almost as a shock that the conditions following the sack of Rome by Alaric and his Goths in 410 marked not a break with, but a return to the past. Outside the imperial frontiers lay the old world, represented on the one hand by the civilized communities of the Near East, and on the other by the Scyths of the Russian steppes and the barbarians of Central and Northern Europe.

The pre-eminence of Rome in so much of Europe, North Africa and the Near East during the early and formative centuries of Christianity is, of course, a factor of great importance, but because it tends to be over-emphasized, it may be useful to consider the background to the exceptional circumstances in which the first Christians practised their religion. In Europe they were due to the existence of the Roman Empire itself which, while it provided means of communication whereby missionaries could travel with more ease and speed than at any other time in history, impeded the spread of the Gospel by intermittent repression and by the tight military control which it exercised over its frontier provinces. In the East, where Rome was faced, either by choice or from necessity, with a less static military situation and with provincials whose existing political and social systems were not readily forced into the Roman mould, Christianity was correspondingly freer, to the later benefit of the whole Church.

The difference between political conditions in the East and the West during the heyday of the Roman Empire may best be explained in terms of historical geography.

The Mediterranean Sea has always been a potent factor in the spread and development of European cultures and civilizations. Almost land-locked and with fine natural harbours, it provides the most direct means of communication between the peoples inhabiting its shores. Moreover, a generally stable climate coupled with a physical similarity between the lands that surround it make the whole area a compact geographical entity, with its limits defined by mountain chains in the North and by the African deserts to the South.

Man's progress from simple food-gathering to a farming economy and, onwards from there, to the establishment of cities, began in the Near East, and so almost throughout antiquity the advance of material progress in the Mediterranean basin was from East to West. Certainly this is true of the introduction by settlers from the Aegean of Neolithic cultures in the Central and Western Mediterranean, and considering the long distances involved relative to the transport then available, the spread of the new ideas and techniques was extremely fast. Outside the Mediterranean area progress was naturally slower, through the Balkans and Danubian lands to Northern Europe for example; and slower still to Atlantic Europe by way of the Iberian peninsula. Later, the dissemination of cultures based on the use of bronze weapons and implements followed a similar geographical trend, though anomalies were inevitable as poorer communities continued to use stone side by side with their more prosperous metal using neighbours. Even greater of course was the disparity in technical progress and material comfort between the cities of Crete or Mycenaean Greece and the contemporary settlements of the Central and Western Mediterranean and, *a fortiori*, with those of Central, Northern and Atlantic Europe. Nevertheless, by the middle of the second millennium B.C. trade relations between the Aegean and barbarian Europe were regular and constant. Amber was imported from Jutland, by way of the Brenner Pass and the Northern Adriatic shore; copper and gold came in from Transylvania. Settlements were established in the Aeolian Isles, Sicily and (very likely) Sardinia for the trade in tin, which was probably carried by sea from Cornwall and Brittany to the mouth of the Loire, and thence by river and land transport to the southern coast of France near Marseilles. In return the merchants of Mycenae traded brilliantly coloured faience beads to adorn barbarian chieftains and their ladies (in death as in life) all over Europe. All, or almost all, this exchange of goods must have taken place through middlemen, yet the find of Aegean beads in a Wessex cemetery brings vividly to mind the long and devious route by which they passed from the clear bright sunlight of the South to the sterner weather of the English Channel; and so to Wiltshire, where Crete, Mycenae, Tiryns and Troy were no more than travellers' tales.

The Dark Age that followed the fall of Mycenae strained to the limit, but did not break the continuity of relations between the Eastern Mediterranean and Central and Northern Europe, and the new post Mycenaean economy based on the use of iron gradually made its way northwards and westwards, as a knowledge of bronze had done a millennium before. In Greece, more efficient agricultural methods led to an increase in population and, stemming from it, a land hunger that could be satisfied only by emigration. Thus began a great exodus of younger sons, landless peasants, merchants and adventurers from all the major cities of the Hellenic world, westwards to the lands of the Mediterranean litoral, and through the Helles-pont and Bosphorus to the Crimean and Black Sea shores. Linked by kinship and religion with their mother cities, these colonies were not isolated outposts or simple trading stations, but took their place as independent members of a Hellenic Commonwealth that stretched from the Euxine to Cyrene, Sicily and Southern Italy, and even as far west as Massilia in Gaul. Trade with their barbarian hinterlands was of course very important, since it enabled the Greeks to dispose of their surplus production, and at the same time to engage in the lucrative business of retailing to the civilized world the raw materials bartered, or even sometimes sold for coined money, by the natives.

The presence of the Greeks so close to their own territories gave to the peoples of the Central Mediterranean, to the Celts of Southern Europe and even to the Scyth nomads farther East a taste for the luxury goods that only the newcomers could supply. In Sicily, Southern Italy and Cyrenaica the local populations became progressively Hellenized, while Greek pottery has been found as far afield as Northern France, Germany and Russia. These finds probably prove little more than the popularity of Greek wines and oil; on the other hand, the discovery of the magnificent bronze *crater* and its associated black-figure pottery at Vix, near Chatillon-sur-Seine, show that *objets d'art* of the highest quality were not beyond the appreciation of a Celtic queen of the late sixth century B.C. It was this familiarity with the products of classical civilization that made the wealthier classes in Gaul and Britain so amenable to the imposition of a 'Roman way of life' some five hundred years later.

Yet the Mediterranean was never a Greek preserve. In North-west Africa and Southern Spain, in Western Sicily and in Sardinia, the influence of first the Phoenicians and, later, the Carthaginians was generally supreme; so too, in its own more limited sphere, was that of the Etruscans in Central Italy. Rivalry was intense, but none of the three powers ever succeeded in establishing an absolute supremacy, and in the long run it was Rome that emerged as the victor not only of Carthage and Etruria, but of Greece herself. The seeds of a unified Mediterranean empire had already been sown; it was only by a historical accident that Rome was able to reap the fruit, and for the first time to transform by force a geographical possibility into a political reality.

At the dawn of Christianity, Rome had already pushed the imperial frontiers in Europe far beyond the natural limits of the Mediterranean area. In the North-west the legions had advanced from the Rhone valley over the Massif Central to the plains of Northern Gaul, and were established on the shore of the Channel, the last natural barrier to the conquest of Britain. North of the River Po, after a series of victorious campaigns, they were now masters of the Alpine passes through which Brennus, Hannibal and, more lately, the Cimbri and Teutones had menaced the Italian motherland. The German wars of Augustus had proved a disastrous failure, and here Rome had fallen back on a policy of containment behind the river barriers of the Rhine and Danube, a wise decision, since a frontier on the Elbe would have placed an intolerable strain on the manpower and financial resources of the Empire.

None of the newly won provinces played a very important role during the Early Christian period, since so long as Roman power remained relatively stable, the traffic in ideas as well as in the material trappings of civilization passed, by and large, up a one-way road from the Mediterranean to the North and North-west. Indeed for centuries, the peoples of the Western provinces lived in a state of suspended animation, and it was not until the barbarian menace had put an end to security under Rome that they began to breathe, painfully enough it is true, but independently again. In 296, Constantius Chlorus could be still hailed in Britain as *redditor lucis aeternae*, but the eternal light was already flickering. It flared up uneasily again in the fourth century, but was only truly rekindled after the collapse of Roman power in the West, and then most brilliantly in lands that the legions had never penetrated. It was then that Ireland became, as Liam and Máire de Paor have put it, 'the last and strangest conquest of Imperial Rome'.

Yet it was not Rome, but the Church with her inherited genius for organization that was soon to be the only effective link between the old Mediterranean lands and Atlantic Europe. St Ninian and St Patrick, as they set out from the monasteries at Tours and Lérins to convert the Picts and the Irish, were certainly aware that they were missionaries of the Roman Church. It is unlikely that either would have under' stood that their journeys to Celtic lands marked the revival of a prehistoric pattern that had been interrupted for a few centuries by an aggressive Mediterranean power.

This is not, of course, to deny that Rome was the instrument whereby Christianity first reached Western Europe; like Mithraism it was almost certainly introduced by soldiers who had seen service in the East, and the persecutions in Southern Gaul under Marcus Aurelius which resulted in the martyrdom of St Blandina and her companions in the arena at Lyons show how firmly entrenched the Faith was there in the second century. Further north and in Britain it does not seem to have taken so firm a hold, at all events before Constantine, to judge from the scanty archaeological record that survives. Above all we look in vain for signs in the Western Provinces of the individualism and strongly marked local characteristics that distinguished the life and art of the Early Church in the East.

In Asia the progress of Christianity in its earliest phases was conditioned no less by geographical considerations than it was in Europe; but whereas in the Western Provinces Rome imposed a certain rigidity and uniformity on the growing Church, in the East its hold was far less secure—sometimes even precarious—and the spread of the new religion among peoples civilized many centuries before the foundation of the City was set to a different tempo. In Europe, missionaries of the Gospel, soldiers and merchants for the most part, travelled along the network of metalled roads radiating from Rome; in the Near East, where the barriers of mountain range and river had long ago been minimized as obstacles to military and commercial expansion, they followed not only the main roads, but also the age-old, well-worn caravan routes that, then as now, took little account of distance or political frontiers. Thus, in Europe the establishment of the Faith outside the areas effectively controlled by Rome was a near impossibility; in the Orient, however, Christian communities flourished beyond the imperial frontiers, and by their vitality and independence influenced the life of the whole Church. This influence was particularly marked in the field of art, since the Near East was open to penetration from the land mass of Asia no less than from the Mediterranean. There was then in the Orient a far greater flexibility than there was in Western and Atlantic Europe, where almost every institution and fashion, political, religious or artistic, depended on the encouragement or toleration of Rome. It should not, however, be forgotten that life in the City itself was being progressively penetrated by Oriental influences, to the great disgust of conservative Romans who saw in the conversion of many of their fellow-citizens to Eastern cults and mystery religions a presage of Rome's decline. Christianity, by reason of its exclusive claims and its rejection of Emperor worship (which for differing reasons was a common bond of loyalty to Rome in both East and West), was particularly abhorrent.

During the first three centuries of the Church in the East, Rome controlled the larger part of what is nowadays described as the Near East, most notably the Anatolian peninsula, Syria, Palestine, parts of Arabia, and Egypt. But while in Western Europe there was for a long time no effective threat to her security, in the East Rome was confronted with another world power, the Kingdom of Parthia, which occupied the greater part of the eastern territories which had once belonged to the Persian Achaemenids and, later, to the Macedonian Empire of Alexander the Great.

Persia had played a vital role in the life of the Near East for many centuries before the Roman *Drang nach Osten*. Politically at her zenith under the Achaemenids, her geographical position, as half-way house between the East (properly so-called) and the Western world, ensured her importance to any prospective world conqueror. To the South-East her frontier marches with Baluchistan, to the North with the Russian steppes. Westwards lies Armenia, while to the South-west, across the Zagros range, are Elam and Mesopotamia, linked in its turn across the Syrian desert with the Semitic coastlands of the Eastern Mediterranean. Seen on a map Persia has the appearance of an impregnable fortress; in fact her northern frontier is vulnerable, and in antiquity it offered fairly easy access to the nomads of Central Asia. Numbered amongst these were the Parthians who, when they could not be contained, soon settled down to a civilized existence based on that of the conquered, just as did Theodoric and his Goths in fifth-century Italy, and the Seljuks and Mongols in Persia during the Middle Ages.

The destruction of the Achaemenid armies by Alexander the Great was followed almost at once by the disintegration of the empire that the Conqueror had inherited from his defeated enemy. Due largely to the jealousy, faction and internecine strife that broke out between Alexander's successors, the internal decay of the empire was further hastened by the abandonment of the King's guiding principle of equal rights and duties for

Macedonian and 'barbarian' alike. Bactria, stretching from the Afghan Plain to the north of the River Oxus, and the farthest outpost of Hellenism in the Near East, was the first territory to be lost to the Seleucids. Its defection in the mid-third century B.C. was no small tragedy in itself, but was soon followed by a heavier blow, the Parthian invasion of Northern Persia. By origin Scythians from the steppes between the Sea of Aral and the Caspian, they crossed the trans-Caucasian mountains and occupied the territory of Parthia, south of the present frontier between Russia and Persia. From Parthia, with whose name they were henceforward to be identified, they advanced steadily if slowly westwards and south-westwards. Progress was slow if only because the late subjects of the Seleucids were under-standably reluctant to accept a new master so soon after shaking off the domination of the old. Individual Seleucid princes sometimes put up a spirited resistance, but the victories of Mithradates I and, two generations later, of Mithradates II were decisive, and put an end in the second century B.C. to the pretensions of the Macedonians to rule the Near East.

In the meanwhile Rome, which had assumed the enviable role of *tertius gaudens* in the struggle between the Seleucids and the Parthians, appeared unaware of the new menace to her Asiatic possessions. Brash and inexperienced in her dealings with the Old World, the Romans in 92 B.C. almost con-temptuously brushed aside an offer of alliance by Mithradates II, a monarch whose empire stretched beyond the Indus and who, some twenty years before, had made a commercial agree-ment with the Emperor of China. For such diplomatic blunders Rome was to pay a bitter price in the humiliation at Carrhae in 53 B.C., when the victorious Parthians carried back the Roman standards in triumph to Ctesiphon.

With the Parthian invasion of Syria and Palestine, the affairs of the Romans now went from bad to worse, and although Antony made strenuous efforts to restore the position, it was left to Augustan diplomacy to secure the return of the Roman prisoners and standards in 20 B.C. In Rome itself the temple of Janus had twice been closed (in 29 and 25 B.C.) as a symbol of peace at home and abroad, and in 9 B.C. the Ara Pacis Augustae was solemnly dedicated. So it was that at the beginning of the Christian era, with a Roman nominee on the throne of the buffer-state of Armenia, an uneasy peace brooded along the frontiers of the rival empires, and at the first Pentecost among the 'Jews, devout men from every nation under heaven' were 'Parthians, Medes and Elamites'.

The infiltration of Oriental cults and mystery religions into Rome during the centuries that preceded and followed Christ's birth has already been mentioned, and it is true to say that at few other periods of history has religion been a matter of such interest and speculation. The significance of life and the possibility of personal immortality preoccupied the minds of thinking men, and nowhere more so than in Rome. There the old religion, based on the twin foundations of *pietas*, whereby a man paid due respect to the patriotic virtues and the traditions of his race and family, and *religio* which demanded the fulfil-ment of his pledged word, was an impersonal and, con-sequently, cheerless creed. Great weight was also given to the scrupulous performance of religious rites as laid down in the Fasti, but the magisterial priests who performed the ceremonies did so as representatives of Rome; they were in no sense mediators between individuals and their gods. The gods them-selves (many of them already identified with the Greek Olympians) gave names to various aspects of human behaviour or natural forces without demanding too rigorous a standard of morality in return for their favours. The educated citizen accepted them with scepticism, though the peasant long remained devoted, even after the establishment of Christianity, to the godlings and genii of the countryside. It was comfortable and tolerant deities like these that the Roman exported to the provinces of Western and Atlantic Europe, where the natives were ready enough to welcome them. Local gods were often enough interchangeable with the members of the Classical Pantheon, and from the Roman point of view it was most desirable that their subjects should feel themselves united with Rome in a common worship. For their own part, several Celtic deities—most notably Epona the mare-goddess and Belenus, patron of the countryside—enjoyed a considerable vogue outside their own homelands; but none survived the critical test of acceptance in Rome itself.

Traditionally conservative, generally suspicious and often contemptuous of foreigners—Orientals in particular—to whom they considered themselves greatly superior, the Romans were slow at first to give official recognition to the cults and mysteries of Asia and Egypt. Such recognition became inevitable, however, as Republican Rome evolved into the cosmopolitan capital of a great empire. A flood of immigrants from all over the East poured into the City; craftsmen and artists from Greece, Alexandria and Asia Minor, Levantine business men and a host of slaves—all came in, bringing not only their alien speech and manners, but new and exotic cults. The soldier too, fresh from campaigning in the East, often returned full of a convert's zeal to propagate his new faith at home, and at last to carry it to the farthest limits of the Roman world. The direct appeal to the senses made by elaborate rites and ceremonial processions was combined with the intellectual satisfaction of a personal religion, and against these philosophical speculation and adherence to the outmoded ethic of a fossilized state religion gave way, gradually at first, but later with ever increasing momentum. Also with the passage of time, purificatory rites whose efficacy had earlier involved no more than the observance of a set form of words and actions without regard to moral worthiness became dependent on the dispositions and intentions of the individual. With this change something akin to a doctrine of Atonement had been established, and man's hope of an eternal reward was the greater or the lesser according to his behaviour on earth. As an almost natural development from this fundamental change of religious climate, the various gods and goddesses became less rivals than partners, local expressions of one transcendental deity to whom all mankind owed allegiance, and a single man could now be priest of more than one religion. It is therefore no more than symptom/ atic of the times in which he lived, that Alexander Severus could give equal honour in his palace to Abraham and Christ as to Orpheus and his own household gods. In such a way was born the religious syncretism of later Roman paganism, a syncretism that culminated in the institution of Sun/worship by the Emperor Aurelian (270–275). The symbolic meaning of this move by the Emperor can hardly have been lost upon the Christians, for in the fourth century the great festival of the winter solstice (25th December) was chosen by them for the celebration of the Sun of Righteousness. Even earlier, in the late third century, Christ Himself had been depicted as the Charioteer of the Sun in the vault mosaic of the Tomb of the Julii in the Vatican cemetery, recalling the imagery of Isaiah:

'His going forth is from the end of the heavens, and his circuit unto the ends of it; and there is nothing hidden from the heat thereof.' Indeed the polemics of some Christian writers against the more outrageous or puerile manifestations of classical paganism often appear to be so much wasted energy, for the horse that they flogged so viciously was moribund, if not actually dead. The poet Prudentius who wrote, towards the end of the fourth century, that 'even then' [in pagan times] 'the road was being prepared for Christ upon His way' showed a greater realism and understanding of his less fortunate fore/ bears than did an Arnobius or a Lactantius.

In the early centuries of Christianity, the three most influential religions of the Orient were those of Cybele, Isis and Mithra.

Of these only Mithra began with an established moral ethic, and so some of its tenets (notably the Persian doctrine of Dualism, whereby the world was conceived of as a battle-ground between Good and Evil) survived the victory of Christianity, and even permeated the beliefs of heretical Christian sects like the Manichees. The mysteries of Cybele and Isis, on the other hand, were originally amoral, but gained in grace as their devotees, probably through direct contact with Christianity and Mithraism, began to feel a need for inward and personal, as well as ritual purification. Each lingered on for a while after the official recognition of Christianity.

Considering the revulsion felt by the insular Roman citizen of the Republic for most innovations, and specially for those imported from abroad, it is curious that one of the most orgiastic of all Oriental cults, that of the Phrygian Cybele, should have been the first to find a home at Rome, and an official home at that. At the close of the third century B.C., towards the end of the Second Punic War, the Sibyls had declared that only the presence of the Mighty Mother in Rome would put an end to a series of portents that was alarming the populace. Hannibal was still on Italian soil, and with him the threat of military disaster. The Sibyls were obeyed, and Attalus I of Pergamum sent from Pessinus to Rome the black meteorite in which it was supposed that the goddess dwelt. The Carthaginian menace was overcome, and in due course a temple was raised to Cybele on the Palatine itself. It was one thing, however, to show appreciation for favours received from a foreign deity; it was quite another to allow Roman citizens to become involved with the barbarous excesses that characterized the cult. So while Phrygian priests and worshippers, isolated in their enclosure, served their goddess unhindered, the Roman people commemorated the arrival of Cybele in Rome by celebrating every April the Megalensia, a feast in her honour, in a manner more becoming their own traditions.

The cult of Cybele sprang from the primitive Anatolian religion which deified mountains, animals, even trees and stones. Cybele was the Lady of the Beasts, the *potnia theron*, especially associated with lions who drew her chariot as she searched for Attis, the grain god, whose death every winter was mourned with elaborate ceremonial. (We shall later see how her lion attendants survived into Christian art, most notably perhaps in the case of the fifth century Adana reliquary, on which a female saint—possibly the Virgin herself—is shown flanked by two of these beasts.) Then, at the time of the spring solstice, when verdure reappears on the plateau and the polished aluminium grey of the wide Anatolian sky gives way to un⁄clouded blue, the feast of Attis resurrection was celebrated. For more than a week before the 24th March the worshippers prepared themselves for the orgies that characterized that day. Sacrifices were offered, and libations poured in blood. Young men, in an access of religious frenzy, voluntarily castrated themselves as the supreme act of self⁄immolation. During the night that followed it was thought that all true believers were mystically united with Cybele and identified with Attis, who rose the next morning triumphant over death. This great event was marked by general rejoicing, characterized by every sort of excess. A day of rest followed, and on the 27th March the savage ritual ended with a solemn procession. Small wonder that the Roman Senate tried to restrict the practice of the cult, but such was Cybele's following under the early Empire that Claudius, thorough⁄going traditionalist though he was, was forced to yield to popular demand and to legalize for all in the city the worship of the Mighty Mother.

Associated with the other rites of Cybele, and later by syncretism with Mithraism, was the ritual slaughter of a bull, the *taurobolium*, which was originally borrowed from the Anatolian cult of Ma⁄Bellona, a goddess closely akin to the Semitic goddess Astarte. At first the purpose of the sacrifice

Plate 48

was to endue the initiate with the physical prowess of the slaughtered animal, but later it was believed to renew spiritual strength also, and could thus be efficacious in the expiation of collective or individual guilt by the ordeal of a single man who submitted to it for reasons of conscience or as the representative of the community. He was stood in a deep pit closed by a grille. Over this grille a bull was led and its arteries severed. Drenched in the animal's blood and 'ghastly to look on' as Prudentius says, the man would then emerge, all guilt washed away, reborn for eternity (*renatus in aeternum*) in something like a travesty of Christian baptism. The words 'reborn for eternity' have a Christian ring, and may possibly have been borrowed by the priests of Cybele from their adversaries.

Compared with the full-toned and strident ritual associated with the cult of Cybele and Attis, the mysteries of Isis and Serapis were set in a minor key. In the religion of ancient Egypt it was Isis and Osiris who, according to Herodotus, were worshipped through Egypt, Isis at this time being identified by the Greeks with Demeter and Osiris with Dionysus. The basic myth which underlay the cult was the murder and dismemberment of Osiris by his brother and enemy Tryphon; the long search for him over the seas by his wife Isis, followed by his discovery and miraculous revival from the dead. However, the cult which later spread so fast and so far throughout the Graeco-Roman world was not purely Egyptian. It had, so to speak, been brought up to date at the end of the fourth century B.C. by Ptolemy Soter in Alexandria, and for Osiris was substituted the new god Serapis, who never-theless seems to have been identified with the original com-panion of Isis from the first. To Ptolemy's Egyptian subjects the recognition of their native gods was a timely political gesture, while for the Greeks, as always curious and avid for novelty, the reformed religion did no violence to their ideas of good taste and sense. In fact it was the perfect compromise for a

Hellenistic Egypt. From Alexandria the cult was adopted by the Greeks of the Eastern and Central Mediterranean; from Magna Graecia it reached Campania, and so inevitably Rome itself, while from Marseilles it travelled up the Rhone valley and so to the frontiers of Atlantic Europe. In Italy it suffered bitter persecution at the end of the first century B.C., probably not so much because of its alleged corrupting influence, as that after the defeat of Antony and Cleopatra at Actium everything Egyptian was held in execration. In A.D. 19, as the result of a scandal involving a Roman matron and a priest of Isis, Tiberius had the goddess's temple destroyed, the priests crucified, and the statue of Isis hurled into the Tiber, but after the Emperor's death, his successor, Caligula, legalized the Isiac mysteries in the city of Rome.

What were the reasons for the extreme popularity of the cult? Quite apart from the ceremonial which marked the two festivals which celebrated the embarkation in autumn of Isis in search of her husband and her discovery of him in spring, the faithful were sustained in their belief by the daily services in her temples. Nor was it a religion for men alone, since Isis and her divine son Horus were specially venerated by women. Ritual purification played a large part in the mysteries, but as Egyptian theology was irrational and chaotic, and since a physical cleansing ritual was all that was demanded for salvation, moral rectitude and chastity were not at first thought necessary in either priest or devotee so long as the age-old formula had been scrupulously carried out. In the moral revival of the second and third centuries A.D., the idea of spiritual cleansing as a prerequisite to salvation and ultimate absorption into the divine so gained ground that Lucius Apuleius could describe in the *Metamorphoses* his initiation into the mysteries in terms of a deeply moving religious experience, in which, in an imitation of Serapis-Osiris himself, he suffered a mystic death and resurrection and thereafter remained for his whole life 'bound to the goddess Isis in chastity and obedience'. But after death, what then? Serapis, identified by the pagans with Zeus and the Unconquered Sun, was also thought to be like Pluto the Lord of the Underworld and Judge of the Dead, and to those who had faithfully served him on earth the god granted immortality of both body and soul and a perfect vision of himself and all the other gods. What the initiate to the mysteries had seen during his lifetime 'in a glass darkly' was to be completely revealed after his death. 'Now I know in part; but then shall I know even as also I am known,' wrote St Paul to the Corinthians. To the votary of Serapis and Isis in the second and third centuries A.D. this sentiment would, *mutatis mutandis*, have struck no discordant note. 'Christ was being thought about,' as Tertullian said of the pre-Christian religions; but in reality, when faced with the infinitely higher moral standard of Christianity and the logic upon which it was based, the mysteries of Serapis and Isis could not, any more than those of Cybele, stand out for long after the emancipation of the Church. Mithraism, the last of the pagan mystery religions to be described here, was a far sterner opponent.

In A.D. 307, when Diocletian proclaimed the Persian god of light as patron of the Empire, the Mithraic religion had been known to the Romans for over three and a half centuries. But although it seems to have made its first converts among Pompey's troops during the campaign against the pirates of Cilicia and Commagene in 67 B.C., Mithraism did not really establish itself in the West until fairly late in the first century A.D. Thereafter it spread like wildfire, especially along the Rhine and Danube frontiers and in the forts of Hadrian's Wall in Britain, for Mithras was, *par excellence*, the soldiers' god. In the Hellenic world it made no impact, probably due to the ancient antipathy felt by the Greeks for all things Persian.

Mithraism, although it had developed individual and non-Iranian characteristics by the time that it was adopted by the

Romans, was essentially deeply rooted in Mazdaism, the religion of Achaemenid Persia, which was possibly reformed about 500 B.C. by Zoroaster. At the head of the Pantheon was Ahuramazda, the sky-god, while the other deities, Mithra among them, shared a subordinate position. The Great King was under the special protection of Ahuramazda and, as his vice-gerent on earth, ruled his empire by divine right. In his reforms Zoroaster apparently introduced into the religion the concept of Dualism, which supposed the existence of two principles, the one good and the other evil, represented respectively by Ahuramazda and his opponent Ahriman. These two were in perpetual conflict; Ahuramazda was supported by the old gods like Mithra, Atar and Apam Napat, the divine elements of Fire and Water, while Ahriman was served by a host of demons. At the end of the world Ahuramazda was to triumph, but meanwhile all men too were involved in the struggle, and were rewarded or condemned in the after-life in accordance with their works.

As the expanding power of Achaemenid Persia moved westwards through Armenia and Anatolia to the Aegean litoral, pure Mazdaism became gradually diluted by its con-tacts with other religions. The *lingua franca* of this western region was not Persian, but Aramaic, and soon, through their proximity to, and close association with the Semitic world, the devotees of Ahuramazda introduced into their still primitive worship the more advanced theology and astrological specula-tion of the Chaldean magi, many of whom had emigrated from Mesopotamia to Anatolia and to the Levant in general. Furthermore, by a syncretic process, Ahuramazda became identified with the supreme Ba'al, or Lord of Syria, Mithra with Shamash, the Sun-god, and Anahita, the great goddess of Mazdaism, with Astarte (Ishtar). This was not all. Mazda-ism also came to terms with the native cults of Anatolia, and in the chaotic period following the collapse of the Seleucid

Empire the petty rulers of Commagene clung tenaciously to a religion which, with a little judicious manoevring, could embrace local gods, identified in their own turn with the recently banished divinities of Hellenism. There is no better example of this syncretism than the rock-relief of Nimrud Dag which shows the meeting between Antiochus I of Commagene (69–34 B.C.) and Mithra with his halo of solar rays directly derived from the Greek Helios. Jupiter of Doliche in Commagene, who was popularly represented in the Roman period as a bearded figure standing upon a bull and brandishing a double axe, was originally an Anatolian mountain-god who had been identified with Ahuramazda under the contrived Greek name of Zeus Oromazdes.

Without Zoroaster's doctrine of Dualism it is unlikely that polytheistic Mazdaism, salted with Semitic theological ideas and Chaldean astrology, would ever have attained the status of a world religion. As it was, in Mithraism the dichotomy between Good and Evil was now stated in something like definite terms. Ahriman, like Satan, was 'a liar and the father of lies'; he and his demons were the cause of all human ills, moral as well as physical, and all men who chose to follow him were foredoomed to hell and, like him, to final annihilation. Mithra, on the other hand, was the spirit of truth, of rectitude and chastity, the champion of Ahuramazda who was not to be bought off with empty ritual or a sacrificial bribe. In fact Mithraism insisted on moral strength as the foundation of a good life, and since this world and everything in it was a battle ground, so every Mithraist was a warrior in the fight against Evil. It is small wonder that the Roman army was a stronghold of the cult, or that the Empire looked kindly on a religion that emphasized the duty of personal subordination to a higher discipline.

Mithraism, which insisted on a higher code of moral behaviour than did any other contemporary religion (with the obvious exceptions of Judaism and Christianity) nevertheless remained earthbound. The seven grades of initiation, the ritual ablution which purged a man of sin, the sacred meal of bread and haôma juice taken by the higher ranks of the initiates—all these have an apparent, yet fundamentally spurious kinship with Christian institutions and sacraments. When it came to the test Mithraism had no historical founder, no exclusive claims, and was as readily absorbed into the Solar Pantheism of Aurelian as it had itself long before readily borrowed from the primitive religions of Anatolia.

It was perhaps unfortunate for the first generations of Christians that the emergence of their religion coincided with the gradual establishment throughout the Roman world of a cult of the Emperor during his lifetime as a being of super-human powers and attributes and who was received into the company of the gods after his death. This cult of a living ruler was no novelty in the Eastern provinces, where it had been practised long before the conquests of Alexander the Great. After his time, Epiphanes—God made manifest—had been accepted as a perfectly suitable *cognomen* for a Hellenistic king a century and a half before Actium. In Rome itself it began with the granting of divine honours to Augustus' adoptive father Julius Caesar, and though during the lifetime of the first *Princeps* it was usually the qualities of Augustus rather than his person that were commemorated, after his death deification followed almost as a matter of course. It was a most prudent act of policy, since it put the position of the Emperor on a sound religious basis and at the same time provided Romans and provincials with a focal point of common loyalty.

In the West, the cult of the Emperor was not only encouraged by the State; it was actually popular. Organization could safely be left to the provincials themselves, and local officials were only too glad to become priests of Augustus (*flamines Augusti*) and to be recognized as good friends of Rome. (Significant in this connexion is the fact that when the British queen Boudicca rebelled against Rome in A.D. 61, the temple of Claudius at Colchester was razed to the ground as a symbolic gesture of defiance.) Furthermore, the provision by the central government of provincial councils (*concilia*) to be attended by delegates of the various communities to celebrate the cult, served to create a consciousness of the political unity of a province.

In the East, the cult was far closer to the worship of the living Emperor as a god, and the *princeps* often found it expedient to allow his statue to be set up with those of other deities, and for temples to be dedicated to him by his enthusiastic subjects. The cult was normally administered by the chief priest of the *Koinon*—the association of cities within a certain area of the province in question.

The attitude of the first Emperors towards their own cult is interesting. Augustus, characteristically, used it as an instrument of policy to such good purpose that its value as an institution was tacitly recognized even by those Emperors to whom personal divinity was distasteful or even comic, as it clearly was to Vespasian, who on his death bed was able to say, 'Dear me! I think that I am becoming a god!' Tiberius and Claudius were both cautious in their assumption of a superhuman role, and were careful to underplay their hand, in Rome at least, where Republicanism was by no means dead. Gaius and Nero on the other hand exploited it to suit their own megalomaniac conceptions of themselves. Gaius was actually prepared to outrage Jewish sentiment by his declared intention of having a statue of himself as Jupiter set up in the Temple itself. However, he did relent, with the characteristically sardonic observation that to lose such an opportunity the Jews must be fools rather than knaves. Domitian liked to be addressed as Our Lord and God (*Dominus et Deus noster*). But however individual Emperors cared to interpret their own cult, it is certain that for the Empire at large it was a most potent factor for unity. The pagan religions were all prepared to submit. Only Judaism and Christianity by their obstinacy placed themselves beyond the pale.

Judaism was not an international religion. Based on the concept that God had revealed Himself to a chosen people who alone had the privileges of inheritance, it had a less direct appeal to Gentiles, who could only share in it by themselves becoming Jews. It is true that their stern morality, their lives ordered according to an unchanging code of God-given laws, induced many people (women for the most part) to embrace Judaism. Generally speaking, however, it was unpopular with, and frequently persecuted by the Romans, whose usual tolerance towards another's religious beliefs was outraged by the uncompromising attitude of the Jews and of their God who would 'have no other gods before Me'.

Christianity has sometimes been described as having started life as a Jewish sect, which suggests that it was no more than an offshoot of orthodox Judaism. As such it may have appeared to contemporary pagans. There is no excuse nowadays for so narrow a view, which ignores the fact that Christianity was designed from the first to be a universal, proselytizing religion without territorial or racial limits. It was this un-Jewish characteristic that made the Christians particularly obnoxious to the Romans, for their God was no less uncompromising than Yahweh in His claim to absolute supremacy, both spiritual and temporal. Further, the Christians, to whom the payment of divine honours to a man was a blasphemy, were seen only as traitors determined on upsetting the imperial applecart. Treacherous also from the Roman point of view was the insistence of Christians on the final doom of Rome, which they nicknamed Babylon, and on the coming of the Kingdom of Christ.

CHAPTER I

The First Three Centuries of Christianity: a Historical Summary

PONTIUS PILATE, appointed Procurator of Judaea in 26, towards the end of the Principate of Tiberius, and recalled ten years later to Rome in disgrace for misgovernment of the Province, would only be remembered today as a poor representative of the Imperial Civil Service, had it not been his fate to be responsible for the condemnation and crucifixion of Jesus Christ. In early Christian art Pilate is usually represented in the act of washing his hands, a personification of his weakness when confronted by the Jewish mob. Yet for the modern Christian this symbolic act of dissociation from blood guilt is perhaps less dramatic than the momentous interview that preceded it—between the representatives of temporal and spiritual authority. It is therefore a strange chance that the earliest surviving text of the New Testament, a scrap of St John's Gospel on papyrus, records some of this extraordinary conversation. The fragmentary page, copied in Egypt in the mid-second century, and originally part of a *codex*, or bound book, is now preserved in the John Rylands Library in Manchester. The reading of the two fragments as parts of St John, XVIII, vv. 31–33 and 37–38 is not in doubt, since wherever it can be checked it conforms with the established text of later *codices*. The passages are these:

Plate 4

'The Jews therefore said unto him, It is not lawful for us to put any man to death: That the saying of Jesus might be fulfilled, which he spake, signifying what death he should die. Then Pilate entered into the judgment-hall again, and called Jesus, and saith unto him, Art thou the King of the Jews?'— and then:

'To this end was I born and for this cause came I into the world, that I should bear witness unto the truth. Every one that is of the truth heareth my voice. Pilate saith unto him, What is truth? And when he had said this, he went out again unto the Jews, and saith unto them, I find in him no fault.'

Both passages, especially the second, would be memorable even if out of context, and it was in the confident belief that 'Every one that is of the truth heareth my voice' that the early Church set out to carry the Christian message to all nations.

The main record of the Church's earliest expansion depends on two divergent, but necessarily complementary literary sources; the Christian apologists and the pagan authors. The outline of the picture presented by both is remarkably con-sistent, though here and there details may be hazy and liable to more than one interpretation, very rarely however in matters of substance. A further feature of Christian history is its con-tinuity from the first century down to our own day; indeed it may be said of the Church that no other institution of com-parable antiquity is so completely documented. The amount of original manuscript that survives is naturally infinitesimal in quantity compared with the volume of works preserved for us by generations of copyists; yet where it does exist, it rarely contradicts, and nearly always confirms the literary and historical tradition. Inscriptions form an important body of original material, but in an era of insecurity, and sometimes of actual persecution, purely Christian sentiments were more often not openly expressed. Veiled and non-committal language was rather the rule.

Just as not so long ago the 'Ancient Britons' were popularly presented in terms of Druids, coracles and woad, so the age of the early Christians was often presented as one of unremitting persecution. Within the Roman Empire this was certainly not the case, and for about two centuries persecution was sporadic, localized and only rarely on a large scale. It was not until the middle of the third century, with the rapid decline of the military situation and the decay of the Empire's political framework, that the Christians were systematically and savagely repressed.

In the earliest years, the Romans saw Christianity as a sect of Judaism. Suetonius, in his life of Claudius, records the expulsion of the Jews from Rome, who 'continually created disturbances at the instigation of Chrestus'. Suetonius apparently did not even realize that Chrestus, or Christ, was not a living Jewish leader of that time. The Jews themselves reacted strongly enough against the new religion which they regarded as striking at the very foundations of their law, and their opposition would have been far more formidable than in fact it was, had they not been temporarily annihilated politically after the destruction of the Second Temple by Titus in 70. There is only a thin line dividing religious from political persecution, since the former is so often a pretext for the latter; thus, this chapter is chiefly concerned with the relations of Christians with the civil power, and first and foremost with the civil power of Rome.

The great fire of Rome began on 18 June 64, and lasted for nine days. Many thought that it had been started by the Emperor himself, and so 'to suppress the rumour, Nero brought to trial and subjected to the most refined tortures those whom the people hated for their crimes and called Christians'. So wrote Tacitus, some fifty years after the event, and went on to record the feeling of compassion that went out from the populace to the 'vast multitude' denounced by convicted fellowChristians who had turned State Evidence. Christianity, again in the words of Tacitus, was an *'exitiabilis superstitio'*, a baneful superstition; yet the sufferings of the victims aroused pity and the 'vast multitude' continued to grow. Not long after the fire—if firm tradition, with no actual evidence to the contrary, is to be believed—Saint Peter and Saint Paul were martyred in Rome.

Not all Roman Emperors were Neros, and for nearly a century after his murder the Christians lived in an unenviable state of suspense and insecurity, with official Rome blowing now hot, now cold, as the political interest of the moment seemed to dictate. To the Christian apologist, particularly if he wrote long after the events he described, the Roman role was all too often over-simplified into terms of calculated malevolence; in fact it is obvious from many pagan writings that it was very often based on a total misunderstanding of the Christian position. The famous correspondence between Pliny, Governor of Bithynia, and the Emperor Trajan suggests two puzzled men, determined to be scrupulously fair towards a reputedly vicious and atheistic sect, rather than two monsters of iniquity. Anyone convicted of Christianity, wrote Trajan, who was prepared to recant should be pardoned, and anony-mous information laid against individuals was to be rejected 'as a bad precedent and out of keeping with the spirit of our times'. Even so, it was in Trajan's Principate that the saintly Ignatius, Bishop of Antioch, was brought to Rome to suffer a barbarous execution in the arena.

But the split personality of official Rome is nowhere better exemplified than in the beautiful account of the martyrdom of St Polycarp of Smyrna, a disciple of St John the Evangelist, who suffered under that most humane of Emperors, Antoninus Pius (138–161). After his arrest Polycarp was called upon by the chief of police to recant. 'Really,' he said, 'what harm is there in saying "Lord Caesar" and offering incense and the rest of it, and so being saved?' To this Polycarp replied: 'For eighty-six years I have served Christ, and he did me no wrong. How am I now to blaspheme my King and Saviour?' A question was answered with a question, and St Polycarp was burned to death. At about the same time a small *memoria*, or shrine in honour of St Peter, was being erected on the southern slope of the Vatican hill in Rome.

It would be wrong to lay any but the ultimate responsibility for the martyrdom of St Polycarp and a few others at the door of Antoninus. In general he followed in the relatively humane policies of his predecessors Hadrian and Trajan, whereby Christians were not to be hunted down nor, if charged, condemned, unless they could be proved to have broken the laws—an escape clause which included refusal to sacrifice to the Emperor as a god.

A long period of comparative peace for the Church was abruptly ended by the accession of Antoninus' adopted son, Marcus Aurelius (161–180). A convinced and practising Stoic and a man of mild, affectionate and loyal disposition, in his dealings with the Christians he proved himself a relentless bigot, and the persecutions which he instituted were all the worse for being directed by a trained and efficient mind. In a life beset with family difficulties, and forced to spend much of it in confronting a growing barbarian menace in military campaigns for which he had no natural inclination, the Emperor saw the Christians, with their supposed atheism, as the *fons et origo* of all his troubles. Whether or not he ever read the *Embassy* of Athenagoras, in which all the usual charges laid against the Christians—atheism, cannibalism and sexual immorality—were more than adequately rebutted, we shall never know. Athenagoras actually dedicated his book to Marcus Aurelius and his son Commodus as philosophers, no less than as Emperors, at some time between 176 and 180, towards the end of Marcus' Principate, but the violence of the persecution did not abate with his advancing years. Justin Martyr, the apologist, was a notable victim of the earlier period, but the worst persecution of all was reserved for the Church in Gaul in 177, when Blandina, a slave girl, and her companions were executed at Lyons with a sadism that can have few parallels in human history. To the victims, whose belief in the resurrection of the body was well known to the authorities, even the rites of burial were denied, and their charred remains were hurled into the Rhone as if thus to deprive them of the hope that had fortified them in their sufferings.

Against a background of such horrible events, the advance of the Church nevertheless steadily continued, and of this the so-called Monument of Avircius is an outstanding proof. By a curious coincidence, the text of the inscription was known before the discovery of the original stone by Sir William Ramsay in 1883, since it had already been quoted in a late fourth-century life of Avircius Marcellus, Bishop of Hierapolis, a city of the Phrygian Pentapolis.

Plate 5

The epitaph, composed by Avircius himself when seventy-two years old, consists of twenty-two hexameters (characterized as 'lame' by Archbishop Carrington, and by Sir William Calder—with a greater sense of justice to a Phrygian of the Christian era—as 'elegant'), in which the bishop described a visit to Rome in the Principate of Marcus Aurelius and his subsequent journeys in the East. Its language is enigmatic, and this was clearly the author's intention. Yet though composed in such a way that it could not have given offence to a pagan, its Christian interpretation causes few, if any, difficulties.

'Citizen of a chosen city I erected this stone in my lifetime that in due time I might have a resting place for my body. My name is Avircius, disciple of a pure shepherd with all-seeing eyes who feeds his flocks upon the mountains and in the plains. He taught me true knowledge, and sent me to Rome to see sovereignty and to look upon a queen with robes and sandals of gold, and there I saw a people on which was a bright seal. I saw too the plain of Syria and all its cities, and Nisibis beyond the Euphrates; and everywhere I found brethren, with Paul in my hands, and Faith everywhere led the way. Every-

where too they gave me to eat of the pure Fish of great size from
the fountain, which a blameless virgin caught, and she gave
continually of this fare to the brethren, having good wine, and
the mixed cup with bread. These things I, Avircius, have
caused in my seventy-second year to be written in my presence.
Let every believer who reads this pray for Avircius. But let no
one put another body in my tomb, and if any one does so, he is
to pay two thousand gold pieces to the Imperial Treasury, and
a thousand more to the fair city of Hierapolis.'

Here then is the last testament of a prominent churchman
who visited Rome to see a sovereign Church. (The reading of
the fourth-century text is followed since, *pace* Ramsay, there is
no evidence whatever on the *stone* to support the reading 'to see
a king and to look upon a queen'. In any case, in view of the
general context, it would be curious that Avircius should have
been sent to Rome to see a persecuting Emperor and his
profligate lady.) In Rome he met the community of the
baptized (the people of the bright seal), and later travelled as
far as Nisibis, finding Christians all the way. St Paul was his
companion, and his faith in Christ led him on. Everywhere he
found the Eucharist being celebrated by the Church (the
blameless virgin), and was given the mixed cup with bread.
Of itself the Monument of Avircius contains little that could
not be learned from a study of the literary sources; but as an
original document it is an important witness to the vitality of
the Church in time of persecution.

Although for a few years Marcus' harsh policy survived him
in the remoter parts of the Empire, it was by accident rather
than design, and under his son Commodus (180–193) the
Christians were generally left to themselves. There was a
notable recrudescence of the terror in the earlier part of Severus'
principate (193–211), especially in North Africa, at Alexandria
and Carthage, but the first half of the third century was

relatively untroubled. The varying eccentricities of Caracalla (211–217) and Elagabalus (218–222) did not lead them to persecute the Church, while the gentle Severus Alexander found a place for Christ, along with Abraham and Orpheus in his private oratory. Of Philip the Arabian it was rumoured that he was actually a convert to Christianity. For a time there had been peace, and the worst was still to come; but the very fact of its coming was a measure of the Church's growing strength, against which not even members of the imperial household were any longer immune.

The rise of Christianity coincided with, even if it did not cause the decay of the old pagan order of things, and it was against a sombre background of military pressure abroad and declining public and private morality that Decius (249–251) assumed the purple after the assassination of Philip. Turning his back on the present, he took the name of Trajan, to emphasize a return to the principles of an Emperor whose moral qualities had become proverbial—'More fortunate than Augustus and better than Trajan' it ran—and sought out the evil, as he saw it, in an attack on Christianity. Of all the Eastern religions that had supposedly undermined the security of the Roman state and the character of its people, Christianity alone had refused to come to terms with orthodox Emperor-worship. In making its acceptance a yardstick of loyalty, Decius concentrated his attack, logically enough, on the leaders of the Church, i.e. the hierarchy. Once eliminated or discredited, the bishops would, he hoped, leave behind them an unorganized rabble to be mopped up at will. Such was the Emperor's reasoning. Yet in the event, Decius' programme was a failure; first, because the hierarchy, and notably Cyprian of Carthage and Clement of Alexandria, saw that their own safety was vital to the survival of the Church; thus, like St Polycarp before them, they did not court arrest or martyrdom, and by putting themselves out of range of the persecutors, continued to direct their flock from a distance. In the second place, the persecution failed because, once the wave of apostasy among the weaker brethren of the rank and file had subsided, a core of resistance remained that was proof against all further trials. This short, but intense period of persecution left a bitter legacy some years later in the schism of the anti-Pope Novatian and his followers, who objected to the generous policy pursued by Pope Cor-nelius and Cyprian, whereby penitent apostates might be reinstated to the full communion of the Church.

The death of Decius in battle against the Goths was followed by two years of anarchy, which provided a breathing space for the harassed Christians. At length, after two military coups, in which the Emperors Trebonianus Gallus and Aemilianus were successively assassinated together with their sons, Valerian, one of Decius' most able officers and a man who had held the important office of Censor during the same Principate, came to power in 253. Like Decius, he initiated a general persecution, marked once more by a special drive against the hierarchy, and St Cyprian himself was hunted down and martyred at Carthage. Further, by a series of carefully graded penal laws he reduced those Christians whom he did not have executed to the rank of second-class citizens, by stripping them of any honours which they might possess and by confiscation of their property. The violence of this persecution has led many to believe that the existence of the cult centre of SS. Peter and Paul at the Basilica Apostolorum on the Appian Way (see below, p. 78) was due in the first place to a translation of the Apostles' relics from their traditional resting places on the Vatican Hill and at the Ostian Gate to avoid the violation of their tombs. How far Valerian's policy might have succeeded had he remained Emperor it is impossible to judge, since in 260 he was taken prisoner by Shapur I of Parthia and died in captivity. His son and successor, Gallienus (260–268), had to face throughout his Principate a disastrous military situation and the threatened collapse of the whole imperial order. In the eastern provinces, quite apart from an invasion of Syria and Cilicia by Shapur, a rash of usurping 'emperors' broke out, while at Palmyra Queen Zenobia embarked on a campaign which was later to detach Egypt and Syria from their Roman allegiance. In Gaul, during the last years of Valerian, the usurper Postumus had set up a rival Empire with all the paraphernalia of its Roman original. Confronted with a situation that would have taxed a far stronger character than he actually possessed, Gallienus was not inclined to add to his difficulties by continuing the persecution of the Christians. Consequently, he issued a rescript whereby freedom of worship and the property confiscated by Valerian were restored to the Church.

For more than a generation the Christians were left in peace, or something like it, and the Church steadily consolidated its position until, as we now know, it became invincible. In Asia Minor and Syria a large proportion of the population—possibly as much as ten per cent—was already Christian, while even in distant Britain the Church had made enough headway by the first half of the third century to merit the reproaches of Tertullian and Origen that it was not yet good enough. In both East and West the internal organization was already taking its now familiar form. A liturgy for the administration of the Sacraments was in full development, while a new art inspired by and dedicated to the service of Christianity was already in being. Even schism and heresy, as a gloomy presage of future troubles, were the concern of the leaders of the Church.

The last general persecution, early in the fourth century under Diocletian (284–305), was fiercer than all the others had been. Yet it was foredoomed to failure, defeated by the very vastness of its scope. Indeed the words so often repeated in the Roman Martyrology, 'who met his death under the Emperor Diocletian—*qui sub Diocletiano Imperatore mortem consecutus est*' are less like a funeral dirge than a triumphant refrain.

After the death of Gallienus, the Principate had become increasingly a purely military office, to be filled (usually with the Army as final arbiter) by one of the successful military commanders of the day. Some of these soldier Emperors, men like Claudius Gothicus, the brilliant Aurelian and Probus, were generals of real stature, and under their rule the Empire won a temporary respite from its difficulties. Aurelian (270–275) also, by canalizing religious observance, other than Christian, into his new cult of the Unconquered Sun infused new life into paganism, for a time at least. However, with the wanton murder of Probus in 282 and the succession by a military coup of Carus, anarchy almost immediately broke out. By 284 Carus and his son Numerian were both dead, the latter as the result of a plot by one Aper, Prefect of the Praetorian Guard. Aper was arrested and ordered to stand trial; but before proceedings had begun, Diocletian, a young Illyrian officer of humble birth but outstanding military capacity, who had been acclaimed as Princeps by the Army in succession to Numerian, ran the murderer through with his spear. Thus, so the story ran, Diocletian fulfilled the prophecy of a Gallic priestess some years before, that he should become Emperor after he had killed a wild boar (*aper*). The army of Carinus, the surviving son of Carus, was still in the field, but after a short campaign, lasting only a few months, it rallied to Diocletian and Carinus was executed. The Emperor now had the allegiance of the whole Army, and with his Principate began a new era in the history of the ancient world. But while the body of the State was rejuvenated, paganism, the spirit which should have animated it, was unequal to the task. It took the genius of Constantine to realize this fundamental weakness in the new order, and to harness to the Principate the only spiritual force well organized enough to ensure the survival of the Empire.

The political and economic reforms of Diocletian were

revolutionary. Rejecting outright any predetermined hereditary principle of succession, he divided the Roman world for administrative purposes into four regions over which he and Maximian ruled as senior Emperors, with two subordinates, Constantius Chlorus and Galerius, named Caesars. Provision was made for the abdication of the Augusti after a period of twenty years, after which the Caesars were to take their place as Emperors, with two subordinates as before. The territorial details are of no concern here, and it is enough to record that while Maximian and Constantius were responsible for the Western Empire, Diocletian and Galerius ruled the eastern provinces. Considering the turbulent nature of the times, it says much for the qualities of Diocletian that, until the time came for the abdication of the two Augusti, all four men kept to their allotted territories without open rivalry or interference. Nor at first was there any animosity towards the Christians, many of whom held positions of trust in the Emperor's household.

The great persecution began in the nineteenth year of Dio-cletian's self-imposed time limit, and curiously enough its origins have never been satisfactorily established. Lactantius, in his vitriolic treatise *De Mortibus Persecutorum*, gives pretexts that seem absurd, while Eusebius is anything but specific on so important an episode of Church history. According to Lactantius, Diocletian was first incensed against the Christians when, in 297, he was consulting the omens about the progress of Galerius' Parthian campaign. On obtaining no response from the augurs, and enquiring the reason, he was told that some Christians present had made the sign of the cross. This is a story unlikely in itself, and in any case a trivial pretext for great resentment; and since the Emperor took no steps against the Church for another six years, it may perhaps be supposed that the story was repeated to drag in the name of Galerius, whom Lactantius particularly detested. In this connexion, it is notable that Galerius was reintroduced as the old Emperor's evil genius when increasingly savage decrees were promulgated against the Christians after the persecution had officially begun at Nicomedia in 303. There was also a charge laid against the Christians of having fired the imperial palace, but reprisals on so vast a scale are inconsistent with what is otherwise known of Diocletian's character from sources less biased than Lactantius. It seems altogether more likely that the decision to launch the great persecution marked the culmination of a period of growing resentment (possibly fostered by Galerius) against the Christians, a resentment for which earlier events provided a pretext.

Diocletian was the first Emperor of Rome to model his official behaviour on that of the rulers of the ancient East, to dress in robes of silk and gold, wear a diadem of pearls, and even to demand prostration before the Imperial Presence. Like Domitian and Aurelian before him, he adopted the style of 'Lord and God'—*dominus et deus*—in the West, while the East (less sensitive than Rome to monarchic pretensions) called him quite simply 'king'. With him began the Caesaropapism—if the word may be used of a pagan institution—that later marked the rule of the Christian Emperors of Byzantium. That Diocletian actually believed himself to be a god is most unlikely, though he seems to have been conscious of a divine mission to safeguard Rome and her Empire. Having escaped persecution under Aurelian, an Emperor of similar pretentions to Diocletian, the Christians need not have felt themselves in imminent danger. In 296, however, an event took place which cast a long and ominous shadow.

In two successive years (268 and 269), Claudius Gothicus had broken the back of the Gothic and Alemannic invaders. Twentyfive years later, although there was no comparable menace, new dangers threatened on the fringes of the Empire. In the West, Britain had been seized by the usurper Carausius, while on the eastern frontiers trouble with Persia was again brewing. Maximian's Caesar, Constantius Chlorus, duly restored the position in Britain, but in 296 Galerius had his fingers badly burned in the Persian campaign, and in that year Diocletian instituted his first persecution of an organized religious body, the Manichees, who combined an acceptance of the Persian doctrine of dualism with heretical Christian beliefs. Following earlier precedents, the Emperor directed his attack against the leaders of the sect, and decreed that they and their sacred books be burned and that subordinates be beheaded, or sent to the mines with the loss of all their property. The real cause of the persecution was anti-Persian feeling, fostered by the military, though Diocletian would also have been swayed by his duty to champion official paganism against the insidious attraction of a new religion, whose adherents, like the Christians, were accused of every sort of vice. The Christian parallel may well have suggested itself to the Emperor at this time, for the Christians, far more than the Manichees, were a menace to the established order. He must have known, without any prompting from Galerius, that they were inflexibly opposed to the State religion and that their Christ challenged his own authority.

The next year Galerius was duly victorious, and an arch was erected in Salonika to commemorate his triumph over the Persians. If Lactantius is to be believed, the incident of the omens took place in the same year, before the issue was decided, and if that were so, Diocletian's anger at so anxious a time would be intelligible enough, though not enough to decide him on persecution.

In 301, only two years before his first attack on the Church, Diocletian issued his famous decree which aimed at pegging the market prices of goods and services throughout the Empire. He had already attempted a currency reform to meet the menace of a steadily creeping inflation, by putting a fixed value on his new gold, silver and copper coinage—but without success. The decree included in its provisions penalties, including death, for exceeding the prescribed maximum prices, but unfortunately it seems to have been given effect only in the East, and too often to have been successfully evaded. Both before and since Diocletian, the persecution of scapegoats has provided a useful diversion of the public mind from economic failure. Unpopular political tenets and religious beliefs are the hallmark of the scapegoat, and the Christians could easily be found guilty on both counts.

Whatever may have been the reason, or reasons, for the action, on 23rd February, the feast of the *Terminalia* in 303, the church at Nicomedia was razed to the ground. The next day a decree was promulgated, requiring all Christians to return to the religion of their forefathers, on pain of the loss of their civic rights, if citizens, and a return to slavery of those who had been freed from that state. As these measures failed in their purpose, the government passed a series of decrees each one more severe than the last. To weaken the resistence of the laity, the clergy were first arrested and imprisoned and, not long afterwards, compelled to sacrifice to the Emperor or suffer death. Under this extreme pressure, some apostatized; recanting under torture was recognized as valid by the authorities, whose chief concern was to break the fidelity of the laity. Finally, before a year was out, the notorious Fourth Decree was issued, whereby all Christians were required to sacrifice or die. By now the persecution was Empire-wide, and both Maximian and Constantius Chlorus carried out the official policy, Constantius, if tradition is to be believed, with less enthusiasm than his Augustus.

In 305, according to the rules which they had laid down for themselves, Diocletian and Maximian solemnly abdicated, in favour of Galerius and Constantius. Diocletian, who was in poor health, did so willingly; Maximian with reluctance. The two new Augusti chose as their subordinates, or Caesars,

Maximinus Daza and Fl. Valerius Severus, for service in the East and West respectively. Diocletian had secured twenty years of stable government, largely through force of personality; with his abdication, the Roman world fell back into chaos.

When Constantius Chlorus became Emperor of the West in succession to Maximian any claim of his son Constantine to act as his Caesar had, quite properly, been passed over. However, when Constantius died at York in 306, Constantine, who was (probably by design) then in Britain, was immediately hailed as Augustus by the troops stationed there. In fact, the death of Constantius automatically entailed the promotion of Fl. Valerius Severus to the rank of Augustus, but instead of appointing a new successor, Galerius, grudgingly accepting the *fait accompli*, recognized Constantine as Caesar of the West. Had matters rested there, the situation might not have got out of hand. Unfortunately for the stability of the Empire, Maximian, who had found the life of an Emperor in retirement little to his taste, returned to active political life, ostensibly to advance the claims to recognition of his son Maxentius who, like Constantine, had been ignored at the institution of the second Tetrarchy. This was nothing less than rebellion against the legitimate Emperor Severus who, on Galerius' instructions, marched to oppose the usurpers. In the event, Severus' troops, many of whom were veterans who had served under Maximian, deserted to their old commander, and in 307 the legitimate Emperor was assassinated. The whole Western Empire was now in the hands of Maximian, Maxentius and Constantine, and a punitive expedition led against them by Galerius had to retire without accomplishing anything. To secure his rear, Maximian had already recognized Constantine as Augustus of Britain and Gaul, and given him his daughter in marriage; but this did not save the old man from being deposed by his son, Maxentius, and in 308 he had so far to swallow his pride as to seek a parley with Galerius in Pannonia, leaving Constantine as undisputed ruler in his own provinces, and Maxentius in Italy, Spain and Africa. Maximian then tried his fortunes with his son⁄in⁄law Constantine, but abused his hospitality by intriguing against him. Finally, in 310 he was executed at Constantine's orders, a figure of universal contempt.

In the West, the Christians actually profited from the dis⁄ orders, as neither Constantine nor Maxentius was in any mood to carry on the persecution, and from 306 onwards the Church enjoyed liberty and peace. In the East, there was no respite. In 308, Galerius, still faithful to the non⁄hereditary principle, appointed one of his generals, Licinius, to be Augustus of the West. Possession being nine points of the law, Licinius' position was purely nominal, and he had to content himself with the single territory of Pannonia. There he emulated his Eastern colleague in the harshness of his persecution, while Maximinus, Galerius' subordinate, usually chose to maim rather than kill the Christians in his own area of jurisdiction. To the Christians it must have seemed that their torment would never end; yet when the end did come, it was not the Church that cracked, but Galerius himself. On 30 April 311, recog⁄ nizing and admitting the failure of his policy, the Emperor issued his famous edict of toleration which restored freedom of public worship and the right to live as a Christian—*denuo Christiani sint*. Five days later Galerius had died of a fearful disease, described by Lactantius with a ghoulish and wholly un⁄Christian glee, and soon afterwards the provisions of the edict were published at the orders of Maximinus, now senior Augustus in succession to Galerius. The great persecution was over, and although it flared up later in the East under both Maximinus and Licinius, it was never again on the same scale, and throughout the succeeding years, until he became sole Emperor in 324, Constantine, the champion of the Christians, increasingly dominated the imperial scene.

With Maximian and Galerius both dead, Constantine

hastened to secure his position as joint Augustus with Maxi-minus and Licinius. Supreme opportunist that he was, he now made it his business to overthrow Maxentius, who as a usurper himself and son of another, had no legitimate title to rule. Before embarking on his campaign, Constantine reached an understanding with Licinius by promising him his sister Constantia in marriage, a diplomatic stroke which was to stand him in good stead when he later quarrelled with Maxi-minus. In 312 Constantine crossed the Alps into Italy and advanced rapidly towards Rome where Maxentius had determined to make his stand. Why he should have so far hesitated it is hard to say, as his troops had fought stoutly in Northern Italy, and he still had an intact army at Rome. Moreover, the city was well stocked, and might well have withstood a siege. In the event, he decided to meet Con-stantine outside Rome, and on 28 October battle was joined at Saxa Rubra, where the naked red *tufa* breaks the surface of the ground a few miles north of the city. Maxentius' army was hurled back to the line of the Tiber, and in the stampede that followed at the crossing of the Milvian Bridge, the Emperor and vast numbers of his supporters were engulfed by the river. When Constantine later entered Rome in triumph, he was hailed by the Senate as Supreme Augustus and ruler of the Western Empire.

The victory of the Milvian Bridge marked the beginning of a new era in history, and in the circumstances it is perhaps natural that it should soon have appeared to Christians as due to a direct intervention of Divine Providence in human affairs. This would explain the popularity of the story reported by Eusebius some twenty-five years after the supposed event, of Constantine's vision the day before the battle of a cross of light in the sky with the words 'In this sign shalt thou conquer!' The story could also be used to rationalize Constantine's choice of the *labarum*, or wreathed Chi-rho, as the Imperial standard.

According to Eusebius, the miracle was vouched for on oath by Constantine. In cases like these, the attitude of scepticism is easily assumed, but perhaps less easily defended. Momentous events in history have at other times been attended, though not necessarily decided, by natural or other phenomena. The eclipse of the moon before the Athenian retreat from Syracuse, the appearance of Halley's comet at the time of the Norman invasion of Britain, and the 'Angels of Mons' in the First World War are examples of such occurrences.

From Rome, where he had now assumed the role of the champion of Christianity, Constantine moved to Milan where Licinius was waiting for him. The two Augusti spent the winter of 312/313 there, and Licinius duly married his colleague's sister Constantia. In 313, the Emperors jointly issued fresh instructions concerning the treatment of Christians in what is usually known as the Edict of Milan. Under the new regulations, Christians now enjoyed full legal rights under the guarantee of the Emperors, and confiscated property was to be restored to them in full.

CHAPTER II

Christian Architecture before Constantine

THE ONLY EXAMPLES of church architecture that either survive from the first three centuries of Christianity or follow the same tradition are striking evidence of the difference in conditions before and after the official adoption by the Roman State of the new religion. The earliest churches were the unobtrusive meeting places for members of a proscribed sect who lived in constant uncertainty of what the future might hold in store; and although some at least were furnished and decorated in a Christian manner, it is fairly certain that the majority would have reflected the absolute simplicity of Apostolic times, a simplicity based not only on the tradition of the first Christian meeting of all in the upper room in Jeru, salem, but on the common sense of avoiding trouble from the civil authorities. Immediately after the Crucifixion, the Apostles had assembled behind closed doors 'for fear of the Jews' and, later, even when they had gained confidence at Pentecost, they still chose to meet away from prying eyes, no longer simply in fear of their own people and religious leaders, but from the representatives of an increasingly hostile Roman government. Throughout *Acts* it is clear that in the period immediately following the foundation of the Church, the Apostles and their converts met for specifically Christian prayers and services only in the private houses of fellow Christians, and the atmosphere of one meeting of this kind is vividly recaptured from the account of St Paul's visit to Troas (Acts xx, vv. 7–8).

'And upon the first day of the week, when the disciples came together to break bread, Paul preached to them ready to depart on the morrow; and continued his speech until midnight. And there were many lights in the upper chamber where they were gathered together.'

Now if the word 'church' is used to mean a place of assembly for the celebration of the Eucharist, the upper chamber just described was one of the first churches in history, even though, architecturally, it would have been quite indistinguishable from the ordinary domestic buildings of the place and period. Thus, in considering the earliest Christian architecture, it should be in terms of the house-church.

No house-church of the most primitive kind has, of course, ever been discovered, since it would not be recognizable if it were; it would have been an ordinary room, used only on special occasions for a religious purpose. On the other hand, as Christianity gained ground, a natural development from this most basic form was the one in which a room or rooms in a house were expressly set aside and furnished as a place of worship, even to the extent of structural alterations and the decoration of the interior with pictures and symbols illustrating specifically Christian themes. It is known that before the Edict of Toleration such churches already existed at Rome, and that many of these were the predecessors of the later *tituli* or parish churches of the city; but of these we know tantalizingly little, since there is no definite archaeological proof that even such well-known structures as the large hall below S. Clemente or the so-called *titulus Equitii* were actually used as churches. In fact, the two examples of the house-church, immediately recognizable as such, are at the opposite ends of the Christian world—at Dura Europus on the Euphrates, and in the Roman villa in Lullingstone Park, near Eynsford in Kent.

The house-church at Dura, built before the middle of the third century, is surprisingly elaborate for its early date. Apart from a portico along the eastern side of a central courtyard, all the other rooms which opened from it seem to have been used

Plate 2

as centres for the principal activities of a Christian community, for the instruction of catechumens, the baptism of the fully instructed and the celebration of the Eucharist. The church proper, which extended along the southern side of the house (and was therefore prudently sited as far as possible from the main door into the street) consisted originally of two rooms which were later converted into a single rectangular hall, with a raised platform, probably for the altar table, at the narrow east end. If the altar was in fact here, it was in contradiction of the later Constantinian practice whereby the celebrant stood, facing eastwards, behind an altar at the west end of the church. In the north-west corner of the house was the baptistery with a font, covered by a baldachino, at its western end. The walls of this room were richly decorated with painted scenes from the Old and New Testaments, symbolizing the Fall and Redemption of mankind. A third room, opening from the east end of the church hall, has been identified as a sacristy, while another, to the west of the central court, was probably used for the instruction of catechumens and neophytes. The priest's quarters were very probably in the upper storey of the house.

This building, apparently devoted wholly to the service of Christianity, is the sole survivor of its kind, but it may be certain that there were many others wherever the new religion had taken root. They are mentioned in some early sources, and late in the second century, when Bishop Avircius travelled through Syria and saw 'all the cities and Nisibis across the Euphrates' it may have been in like surroundings that he met his 'brothers' and partook of 'the mixed cup with bread'.

At Lullingstone, the northern end of a long established Roman villa was sealed off in *c.* 350 from the other domestic apartments and entirely redecorated as a centre for Christian worship; not only, it would seem, for the owner and his family, but for their Christian friends and neighbours also. (This may be deduced from the fact that the entrance to the chapel, by way of a small square vestibule and an oblong ante-room, was outside the house.) The painted wall plaster that has been assembled is convincing proof of the Christian character of the two larger rooms. The southern wall of the ante-room was decorated with a Chi-rho monogram and the letters *alpha* and *omega* in a wreath, while on the west wall of the room identified as a chapel six *orantes* (figures with their hands raised in prayer), each one framed between a pair of columns, were painted above a dado of floral motives. Another wreathed Chi-rho on the chapel's southern wall was visible to the worshipper entering from the ante-room. Although the villa itself was abandoned as a dwelling-house in *c.* 380, the chapel continued in use until the turn of the century, when it was burned out for good. Much simpler than the Dura house-church and considerably later in time, it may surely be thought still to reflect pre-Constantinian conditions in the remoter centres of population in the more isolated provinces.

The house-church, as a makeshift at a time when there was no tradition of Christian buildings on a monumental scale or, at all events, none of which we have any precise knowledge, had no influence on the later basilical architecture of the Church. Architecturally the church at Dura is no more than a house, while the Lullingstone chapel is only part of one; neither of them lend any support to the once fashionable theory that the basilical church might have developed from Roman domestic architecture. This theory was based on the assumption that houses of the Pompeian type were standard during the early Christian era, and that in the *atrium, tablinum* and ornamental table are to be seen the prototypes of the basilical nave and the apsidal recess with its central altar. As long as such houses were almost the only examples of Roman domestic architecture, speculation of this kind was reasonable; but recent excavations at sites outside Italy have shown that a great variety of house plans existed in different parts of the Roman world, so that the theory of a wholesale derivation of the Christian basilica from one specialized type is untenable. Only one example is known, from Merida in Spain, of an early church which seems to be the successor to a house approximating in plan to the Pompeian type, and here it is not at all certain that the house was used as a place of worship before structural alterations, including the addition of an apse to the *tablinum*, and the removal of the *impluvium* to one side of the *atrium*, were put in hand after the emancipation of the Church.

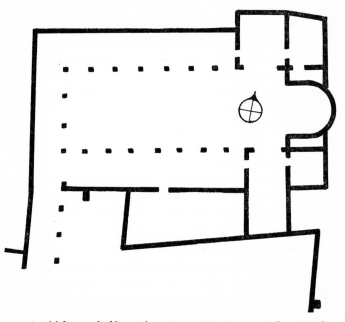

Fig. 1   Apsidal funerary building with porticoes at Marusinac near Salona in Dalmatia. Third century

Nevertheless, in Syria, as a result of local tradition, which for a time even withstood the immediate post-Constantinian trend towards the adoption of the basilical plan, the arrangement, if not the exact form of the Dura house-church did survive. At

Kirk Bizze, in the Jebel el 'Ala, Tchalenko has discovered that a large building, thought previously to be a house, was in fact a single-naved church with a long hall, or *narthex*, on its south side, which itself was entered through the northern portico of a large paved court. (Later, when the basilical church had gradually asserted itself in Syria, an open court to the south was still not abnormal there, and was found in eastern Cilicia also.) At Umm-al-Jemal, in southern Syria, the church was a large complex, of which the basilical hall was a single part.

There is no archaeological evidence for the existence of ecclesiastical architecture on a monumental scale before the Peace of the Church. The small rectangular building at Parenzo in Istria has indeed been claimed as the predecessor of the earlier cathedral there, which has itself been assigned to the Constantinian period; but even if it were, it does not prove that any specialized church architecture had evolved before the end of the third century, since the absolute simplicity of its plan denies it any place in such an evolution.

The apsidal funerary building discovered by the Danish scholar, E. Dyggve, at Marusinac near Salona in Dalmatia, is distinctly more ambitious. The continuous colonnade surrounding a central court and the situation of the tomb within the apse, suggesting the position of the altar in later basilical churches, led Dyggve to claim this building as a *basilica discoperta*, a hypethral basilica in the direct line of development towards the standard church of post-Constantinian times. On architectural grounds this theory is dubious, since it appears to ignore the absence of roofing and of the usual longitudinal emphasis, which are characteristic features of the true basilica. The central court at Marusinac, which is open to the sky, is a negation of roofing, while the disposition of the colonnades round it produces a centralized plan.

Archaeological evidence apart, some literary sources appear

to refer to large churches, other than house-churches, that were built before 311. One passage in the *Chronicle of Edessa* con-cerns a church in that city which was apparently destroyed by flooding in 202; another, in Lampridius' life of Severus Alexander, describes the intervention of the Emperor in favour of some Christians in Rome who wanted to build a church at a site that had been earmarked for an inn by the guild of tavern-keepers. A third, in Lactantius' *De Mortibus Persecu-torum*, contains a circumstantial account of the demolition, during the great persecution under Diocletian in 304, of a church at Nicomedia which was situated on a hill in full view of the imperial palace. That it could be pulled down in a matter of hours does not give the impression of its having been a very substantial building. All the available evidence tends to show that apart from house-churches and, possibly, some relatively undistinguished and more or less temporary buildings designed *ad hoc*, there was no Christian tradition on which architects could draw when the Church attained its freedom.

So long as Dura still provides the only example of a pre-Constantinian church building, it cannot be pretended that anything is otherwise known of their decoration or furnishings, though a few gaps may be tentatively filled by the evidence of a few paintings in the Catacombs and by some inscriptions and reliefs.

At Dura itself, it is most interesting that the carefully arranged religious scenes painted on the walls of the Baptistery are already didactic in tone, and thus anticipate by nearly three centuries the so-called 'Poor Man's Bible', as exemplified by the mosaics

Plates 72, 73

in S. Apollinare Nuovo in Ravenna. The pictures, which illustrate a variety of stories from the Old and New Testaments, are concerned with the theme of man's Fall and Deliverance. Besides these, with their strong doctrinal purpose, the Chi-rho and *orantes* of the Lullingstone frescoes seem almost non-committal, and it may be that this divergence between them is a measure of the greater artistic vigour of the early Church in the East during the formative centuries. It is interesting to note that a synagogue close to the church at Dura is decorated with scenes from the Old Testament, and in a closely related style. It is little larger than the church, but its plan is of a more definitely religious character. But even if (as seems likely) the East took an early lead in the field of Christian art, some at least of the house-churches in the West which have been lost to, or not yet reclaimed by archaeology, must surely have been decorated with scenes as recognizably Christian as those now long familiar from the Catacombs.

Where church furnishings are concerned, the ground is still less secure. Of the altar, the focal point of the Christian liturgy, it is known that it was at first a simple wooden table. In the earliest house-churches a fixed stone altar would have been not only an inconvenience, but unnecessary to the undeveloped form of the liturgy then in use. The use of the table was one of the reasons that the pagans, who largely associated religious worship with a bloody sacrifice, insisted that the Christians were atheists, as Athenagoras (*Embassy*, 13) makes clear: 'Judging piety by the practice of sacrificing, they accuse us of not reverencing the gods of the city in each place. . . . The Creator and Father of this universe needs no blood nor fat of sacrifice nor fragrance of flowers and incense, for He is Himself perfect fragrance, needing nothing to make good defects nor any addition.' In a third-century fresco in the Catacomb of Callixtus, the altar is depicted as a small three-legged occasional table, on which lies the Fish, symbol of Christ and, through Him, of the Eucharist. Wooden altars seem to have gone out after penal times, but their traditional form, with a variable number of legs, was frequently imitated in stone. A type that seems to have been specially popular during the third century was the sigma or semicircular table then being used in domestic *triclinia*, possibly an indication of the general prevalence

65

Fig. 2 *Fragmentary gravestone from Çeltikci in Phrygia, now in the Museum at Kütahya. Third century*

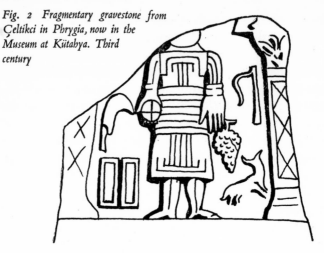

of the house-church at this period. It is, indeed, the kind of table most often portrayed in the earliest Eucharistic scenes from the Catacombs and on sculptured sarcophagi—scenes clearly derived from the idea of the pagan *refrigerium*, or refreshment meal in honour of the dead. In Christian terminology, by a transference of associations, the word was primarily applied to celestial bliss, as it is in the prayer for the dead in the Roman rite, that they be granted a 'place of refreshment, light and peace'. The number commonly shown seated at the sigmatable is seven, a probable reference to the seven disciples who were present at the Miraculous Draught of Fishes described by St John (XXI, vv. 1–13), while the seven baskets depicted in two chapels (A5 and A6) in the Catacomb of Callixtus, recall the Feeding of the Four Thousand in St Mark's Gospel (VIII, vv. 1–9).

Beside the symbolic Fish, the two elements of the Eucharist, bread and wine, are represented by round loaves, quartered by a cross, and either a chalice or a bunch of grapes. In the earliest known example, on a funerary relief from Phrygia, the

Plates 6, 8

primitively carved, severely frontal figure holds in his out
stretched left palm a bunch of grapes suspended from a tau
cross, an early form of the sacred symbol. In his right hand is a
loaf of the type already described. No church plate associated
with the Eucharist has survived from this period.

Fig. 2

While it is disappointing that there is so little archaeological
evidence, it can hardly be doubted that some of the abundant
material surviving from the fourth and, even more, from the
fifth centuries was at least foreshadowed in buildings that have
not yet, and possibly never will come to light. A single example
may perhaps be cited as evidence in favour of this belief. St
Cyprian in the third century states that the sermon which
normally preceded the Eucharist was delivered from a raised
platform (*pulpitum*). If this is true of North Africa, it is likely
that in the East the reading desk of the Jewish synagogue was
already well on its way to becoming the Christian ambo (from
which passages of the Scriptures were read) before the Peace
of the Church. Its presence in the form of a speaking platform
at Kırk Bizze in Syria fairly early in the fourth century certainly
suggests that it existed in the later house-churches at least.
Meanwhile, without further excavation, the question of such
survivals must remain a matter for hopeful speculation.

Christian life in Apostolic times was centred, as it has been
ever since, round the celebration of the Eucharist, and however
elaborate and varied the liturgies that later developed, the
essential act of thanksgiving over the elements of bread and
wine (as described by St Paul in I Cor. XI, vv. 23–26) has
remained unaltered. It was primarily for the Eucharist that
rooms in simple private houses were first set apart, and for the
Eucharist that Justinian raised and dedicated the church of
St Sophia in Constantinople. So, while ecclesiastical archi
tecture may be a subject for archaeological and historical
research, it can only be fully understood in connexion with the
worship that inspired it.

From the accounts of the Synoptic Gospels it would seem that Christ instituted the Eucharist in the course of a religious meal held in common with the Apostles. This meal was not in fact the Pasch, since the Last Supper took place on Maunday Thursday, a full twenty-four hours before the beginning of Passover. Later, however, the times were close enough together to become more or less identified, as also was Christ with the Paschal Lamb (I Cor., v, 7). Such common meals were a regular feature of Jewish religious life, but the Last Supper differed from all others in the manner in which Christ pro-nounced the thanksgiving over the bread and wine before He distributed them to the Apostles. For some decades at least, the religious meal continued to act as a setting for the Eucharist, not only among the Christian Jews for whom the practice was established by tradition, but also among the Greek Gentiles, many of whom before their conversion would have been initiates of mystery religions in some of which the eating of a common meal was a recognized feature. Gradually, though it is not known when the change began, the Eucharist became dissociated from the common meal, and the latter diminished in importance. If the later development of the liturgy is any guide, the separation would not have taken place everywhere simultaneously, and it is likely that the older practice would have lingered longer in Palestine, where it originated, than in the other new centres of Christendom. It is possible that by 112, when Pliny the Younger (at that time Governor of the Asiatic province of Bithynia) wrote to the Emperor Trajan with a request for guidance on the treatment of his Christian provincials, the separation had already taken place. Pliny relied for his information on the reports of apostates, reports that would almost certainly have been accurate in the first place, though obviously liable to misinterpretation by the scrupulous Governor himself. He was told that the Christians met on a fixed day—certainly Sunday—before dawn, and recited a hymn or set formula of words (*carmen*) to Christ as to a god, and also swore to avoid crimes like stealing, perjury and adultery. Later in the day they gathered again to eat a harmless meal together (*cibum communem tamen et innoxium*). Pliny's account is, then, evidence that the Christians met twice on a Sunday, and it is surely certain that one of these meetings was for the celebration of the Eucharist. In the light of later practice, the early morning would seem to be the more likely time for this, which would indicate that the second gathering was for the common religious meal of Apostolic times. It is also possible, though perhaps not so likely, that Pliny's account referred only to the Eucharist, divided as later into two distinct parts. Whichever may be the case, the use of the word *carmen* suggests that the Eucharist was already preceded by a set form of prayers and readings from the scriptures, a practice ultimately derived from the Jewish liturgy and which was later known as 'the administration of the word' or the Mass of the Catechumens (*Missa Catechumenorum*). In the Church's earliest years the Apostles, as Jews, still attended services in the Temple and preached in the synagogues, while at home they prayed together as Christians. Such prayers would have had a Jewish as well as a Christian inspiration, and so too the 'psalms, hymns and spiritual songs' which St Paul likewise enjoined upon the faithful (Eph., v, 19). In the meeting one Sunday at Alexandria Troas mentioned above (p. 58), it is recorded that the breaking of bread was preceded by a discourse from St Paul which lasted until midnight, and it is likely that such a sermon would have included readings from the Old Testament. It is, then, reasonable on many grounds to suppose that the Apostolic and immediate post-Apostolic liturgy would have included Scriptural readings and prayers, and, if so, to infer from later practice (e.g. the second-century liturgy of Justin Martyr), that these preceded the thanksgiving over the bread and wine and the subsequent distribution of the Sacrament. For the rest, it is known that those Christians who gathered for the common meal habitually brought their own food and drink (a custom which may be thought to foreshadow the Offertory later incorporated in the liturgy), and that alms were collected on Sundays. The Kiss of Peace, which in the Roman rite now precedes the Communion, was instituted in Apostolic times, but was not then confined to the Eucharist alone.

From these simple beginnings, the development of the liturgy, as described by Justin Martyr in his *Apologia* and *Dialogus ad Tryphonem*, had made considerable ground not long after the middle of the second century. It appears to have been in two distinct parts, not unlike the present divisions of the Roman Mass into the Ordinary and the Canon. The first, harking back to the synagogue, was the service of the word (*administratio verbi*), and consisted of lessons from the Scriptures, both Old and New, and a sermon followed by prayers; it was concluded by the Kiss of Peace, in this case preceding the Canon, as it did in the later liturgies of Alexandria and Northern Italy. The second, at which only baptized Christians might assist, was the Eucharist proper. This began with an offertory of bread, wine, and water to the celebrant, who then gave thanks over them in an extempore prayer to which the congregation responded 'Amen'. The consecration over, the Sacrament was then administered to the people by the Deacons. At the present time, the distinction between the two parts of the liturgy is not specially marked, since the Eucharist follows directly on the lessons and prayers which were originally intended primarily for Catechumens, penitents and pagan enquirers. In the early Church, however, they could be quite separate, as Tertullian, half a century after Justin, makes clear in his words '*either* the Sacrifice is offered *or* the word is administered', a clear reference to the Mass of the Faithful (*Missa Fidelium*) and the Mass of the Catechumens (*Missa Catechumenorum*). In this connexion, it is perhaps worth stressing that the word '*missa*' did not at first have the meaning now associated with it, but signified only the 'dismissal' of that part of the congregation to which it applied. In the third century, the evidence from North Africa is specially valuable, and both Tertullian and St Cyprian enlarge on liturgical details many of which are still familiar in the Roman rite. As will be seen later, the bond between Carthage and Rome was nearly always a close one. From Tertullian we know that readings from the Epistles and Gospels were an established part of the Mass of the Catechumens, and St Cyprian was familiar with the opening words of the Preface: 'Lift up your hearts— *Sursum corda!*', with its response 'We have lifted them up unto the Lord—*Habemus ad Dominum!*'

With the house-church at Dura in mind, it is tempting to speculate on the state of the Syrian liturgy in the mid-third century, but there is no direct evidence, and Chrysostom's account of the Church at Antioch in his time (370–398) is far too late to be instructive. It will surely not have lagged behind the liturgies of the contemporary Christian world, and from the remains of the church itself we have certain proof of the importance attached to Baptism and, *a fortiori*, to the Eucharist. For the rest, we may assume a congregation conversant with both the Old and New Testaments, for the wall paintings were surely not intended more as a means of instruction than as familiar and well-beloved subjects for meditation.

Christian building before Constantine was not, of course, confined solely to churches any more than it has been from his time onwards. There were few, if any, separate baptisteries, since the baptismal rite does not of itself demand an elaborate architectural setting. Christ had Himself been baptized in the Jordan, and the third-century wall paintings in the Catacomb of Callixtus suggest the primitive simplicity of the Gospels and St Philip's baptism of the Ethiopian. Dura, however, shows how much importance was rightly attached to the Bright Seal, as Avircius described it, and baptisteries as a part of more elaborate house-churches may well have been not abnormal.

The worthy commemoration of the dead, and specially of the martyrs, was very early a matter of moment to the growing Church, and provided the occasion for architecture of a sort, even though not necessarily of the most impressive. Among such monuments, the so-called Shrine of St Peter, discovered in the course of the Vatican excavations carried out during and after the 1939–1945 War below the crypt floor of St Peter's in Rome, is of unique and outstanding interest. Thus it deserves a more detailed treatment and a fuller discussion than would be admissible for a similar funeral shrine of less extraordinary associations. Since the possible implications of the discoveries have been sometimes exaggerated beyond what the evidence will bear, Professor J. M. C. Toynbee has rightly insisted that 'no doctrinal issue whatever is involved in so relatively secondary a question as the precise site in Rome of St Peter's burial', and in fact no proof exists that the small second-century *aedicula* found by the excavators was used to mark a tomb. However this may be, and however much scholars may dispute the interpretations made by the excavators of their results, as published in their *Report* of 1951, it is generally conceded that the *aedicula* may be identified with the *tropaeum*, or trophy of St Peter, which was seen by one Gaius, a priest, in about 200. Moreover, it is indisputable that when Constantine built the first church of St Peter in Rome, he chose a site already hallowed by a tradition of almost two centuries. In fact, so strong were the associations of the *aedicula* with the Apostle, that the Emperor had it incorporated in the place of honour, in the centre of the chancel of the new basilica.

Superficially, the Shrine of St Peter is fairly reminiscent of some pagan funerary monuments. These, however, were usually incorporated in a larger tomb structure rather than built as memorials on their own account. Considered in detail, the

Fig. 3 The memoria of St Peter on the
Vatican hill, as restored by G. U. S. Corbett

aedicula has many curious features which cannot be explained in the light of contemporary pagan usage, and these are bound up with the earlier history, as revealed by excavation, of the area in which the Shrine was built.

Although the excavations have already been described in the Vatican *Report* and their results analysed in numerous publications, the subject is of such interest that I have felt it necessary to include a summary here. As will be apparent, I am particularly indebted to the publications of Professor Toynbee and Mr J. B. Ward-Perkins.

At the beginning of the Christian era, the southern slope of the Vatican hill was still open country in which a few inhumation burials had been made. A century and a half later, although the rest of the site had become a crowded cemetery,

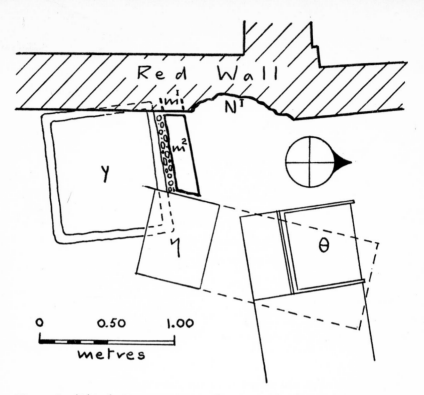

Fig. 4 Area 'P' in the Vatican Cemetery with its associated tombs and structures in the mid second century

one area, called Campo 'P' by the excavators, seems to have been systematically avoided. It was at the western end of this area that the *aedicula* was erected, probably between 160 and 170.

Before that time this area had been partially defined by some inhumation graves, of which it is known from the archaeological evidence that none can have been earlier than the second half of the first century A.D. nor later than the middle of the second. The upper limit of between 69 and 79 is determined by the maker's stamp on a tile used in the construction of Grave θ, which itself was contemporary with, or perhaps very slightly later than Grave γ; a third grave, η, dug after the level of the ground had been artificially raised, was later than either

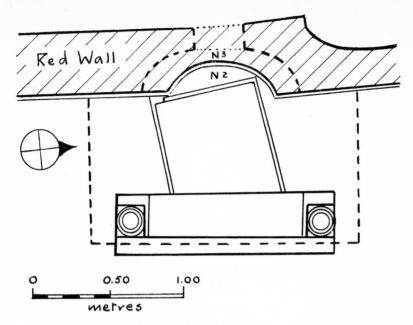

Fig. 5   *Ground plan of the first* memoria *of St Peter*

of these, but was still earlier than the Shrine, since it passed
below the floor slab of the *aedicula*. At some time, also between
the digging of the earlier graves and the building of the Shrine,
a wall, Mɪ, running approximately from west to east, was
constructed south of and approximately parallel to the later
site of the *aedicula*. Whether it was originally intended to define
the northern limit of Grave γ, or to prevent the spill of earth
into Campo 'P', as the excavators supposed, is not proved one
way or the other. It is however certain that this wall did later
mark the true southern limit of the *aedicula*. Since γ, η, and θ
are all inhumation graves, they have been claimed by some as
Christian; but cremation, though a normal pagan usage at
that time, was not universal, and Jews as well as Christians
regularly buried their dead. In fact γ seems to be a pagan grave,
while η and θ may be, but are by no means certainly Christian.
The lower dating of the graves and, incidentally, of the Shrine

75

itself, is bound up with the construction of the so-called Red Wall which defined the western limit of Campo 'P'. This wall is of one build with a tomb area under the floor of which was a drain constructed partly of tiles; among these were five with stamps to be dated to the Principate of Antoninus Pius or, to be more precise, between 147 and 161. Shortly after the completion of the Red Wall, another wall, M2, was built on the exact line of the earlier M1. This new wall marked the southern limit of the Shrine, while a fresh inhumation grave, which was exactly contemporary with the Red Wall, defined the Shrine area to the north.

The *aedicula*, which backed into the Red Wall and therefore faced eastwards, consisted of three superimposed niches, of which only two (N2 and N3) would have been visible above ground level. These were separated by a single projecting slab

Fig. 3

of travertine resting on two colonnettes. Corbett's reconstruction shows the upper niche crowned by a pediment, supported by two more colonnettes; but these features, although following the usual design of contemporary pagan monuments of the type, are conjectural. N1, the lowest of the three niches, was below ground and, as distinct from N2 and N3 which were of one build with the Red Wall, was apparently cut into its foundations very soon after their completion. Furthermore, a closure slab in the floor of the *aedicula* was set at a distinct angle to the main axis, an angle corresponding exactly to the alignment of M2, the wall defining the southern limit of Campo 'P'. The builders of the Shrine were, therefore, much concerned to preserve a detail of orientation at the expense of normal architectural symmetry.

The excavation of the central area, accomplished under extremely difficult conditions, led to the discovery of a small rectangular chamber, below the floor of which, in a deposit of earth sometimes as much as two feet eight inches in depth, was a large collection of coins dating from the first to the fourteenth centuries. Though few of the coins were earlier than the fourth century, they are still evidence of a continuous cult at the same spot for over a millennium. How the coins were deposited is not known; there must have been some opening or grille through which they were dropped from above.

A further discovery, in the lowest level of the *aedicula*, may partially explain the construction of N1 in the foundations of the Red Wall. Below this niche, and almost in the centre, the excavators found a fissure extending westwards through the thicknesss of the foundations. In the earth that filled it was a pile of human bones which they describe as having belonged to a person of 'advanced age and powerful physique'. An analysis was promised, but despite the long time that has elasped since their discovery, no further account of these bones has yet been published.

There is no evidence that the Shrine was built above a grave; still less that the bones found in the excavation are those of St Peter. On the other hand, the decision to cut a niche which was never intended to be seen does suggest a sudden alteration in the preconceived plan of construction of the *aedicula*. Toyn-bee and Ward-Perkins have very reasonably suggested that this alteration may have been occasioned by the discovery of a burial by the workmen engaged in the construction of the Red Wall which, rightly or wrongly, they interpreted as being that of St Peter himself. Such a reading of the evidence would also well accord with the otherwise unexplained fact of the evident importance attached to the exact orientation of the closure slab of the *aedicula*.

From what we know of it the Shrine is not specially impres-sive architecturally, though its two visible niches with the intervening slab of travertine are certainly abnormal. The posi-tion of this slab, about four feet ten inches above the floor, seems far too high to be considered as an altar stone, and it may well have been used rather as a *prothesis* or table for offerings.

The arrangements below ground are unique, and only explic, able as due to exceptional circumstances. The Shrine has, in fact, no parallels.

The last type of primitive Christian building to be described here is that used for the celebration of *refrigeria*. Only two examples are known, of which the more famous is the so-called *triclia* below the church of S. Sebastiano on the Appian Way just outside Rome. Its discussion at this point is apposite, since for several centuries the site was associated with the cult of SS Peter and Paul, and the church, before its rededication to St Sebastian, was known as the Basilica Apostolorum.

A regular feature of funeral practice in pagan Rome was the honour paid to deceased relatives and friends on the anniver, saries of their death in the form of a *refrigerium* or refreshment meal. The celebration was characterized by a gathering at the tomb, followed by a good deal of food and drink, and so was not unlike an annually recurring 'wake'. Like so many unobjectionable elements of paganism, the *refrigerium* was retained by the Christians, to some of whom it may have suggested a symbol of the Eucharist. At all events, *refrigeria* are a common subject for Catacomb frescoes and reliefs on early sarcophagi. The refreshment meal was not necessarily a sober affair; indeed the Christians themselves were sometimes taken to task for allowing such functions to get out of hand, and there is more than a hint of riotous behaviour in a relief from the sarcophagus of Baebia Hermophile at Rome, where excited Plate 8 gestures and a raised cup do much to counteract the Christian effect of loaves signed with a cross, and a sigma-table seating seven. Another contemporary relief from a fragmentary Plate 6 sarcophagus represents the same scene, but with an obvious difference of approach and a feeling for its spiritual significance.

If the anniversaries of ordinary Christians were so celebrated, how much more honour was due then to those of the Saints and Martyrs! According to tradition, SS Peter and Paul, the

greatest of them all, were buried at the places of their martyr,
dom, on the Vatican hill and at the Ostian Gate respectively;
moreover the Vatican excavations have shown that the first site
was certainly associated with St Peter from the second half of
the second century. Yet, when the joint feast of the Apostles
was instituted, probably for the first time on 29 June 258, it was
celebrated not at Rome but at the site on the Appian Way.
There too, not long afterwards, a small one-roomed structure
was erected to provide accommodation for pilgrims celebrating
refrigeria in honour of the two Apostles. Of the different
answers advanced to explain this shift of emphasis away from
Rome, the most popular is that the remains of SS Peter and
Paul were translated during the persecution of Valerian from
Rome to the site on the Appian Way, and were later returned
to their original graves in the time of Constantine. Against this
there are a number of reasonable objections, but the association
of the two Saints with the site is, whatever the reason, not in
doubt. In the second half of the fourth century, Pope Damasus
set up his famous metrical inscription near the Basilica
Apostolorum, in which he stated that the Apostles had once
'dwelt' there—whether in life or death it is impossible to say,
and both interpretations are possible.

Against this fascinating, if illusive historical background,
the undistinguished architecture of the cult centre naturally
suffers. Opening on to a courtyard, in which stood a throne-
like structure, possibly used by pilgrims for depositing their
offerings, was a single covered room with a continuous bench
round its walls. Here the *refrigeria* were celebrated, and here, on
the walls, were scratched pious invocations to SS Peter and
Paul by name.

CHAPTER III

Christian Art before Constantine

PARTIALLY DUE TO an accident of survival, but also to the generally unsettled political conditions that prevailed during the first centuries of Christianity, the art of the period is nearly all funerary. Decorated churches there certainly were, but of these only the wall paintings of the Dura house-church so far survive to remind us of the surroundings in which the first Christians worshipped. For the rest, monuments to the dead, inscriptions, frescoes and sculptured sarcophagi form the main body of evidence for the art of Christianity before Constantine.

In a sense, this is as it should be, for the Christians of the period sometimes lived very near to death, not only as members of a sect liable to be proscribed without warning, but also because death, whether natural or by martyrdom, was the gate-way to Heaven, the goal towards which the whole Christian life was directed. Life itself, in the sense of sharing in the activities of a largely pagan community, was largely irrelevant, though this does not mean that the average Christian, as opposed to a minority who actually courted death by martyr-dom, was normally anything but circumspect. Even St Poly-carp, Bishop of Smyrna, 'waited to be betrayed as also the Lord had done, that we too might become his imitators, not thinking of ourselves alone but also of our neighbours . . . For this reason, brethren, we do not commend those who surrender themselves, for the Gospel does not enjoin us so to do.' So it is that the individual men and women who stare at us from the central medallion of their sarcophagi are not avowedly or obviously Christian. It is only their association with the symbols of the Redemption or with scenes that illustrate Christ's promise of an eternal reward for the righteous that differentiates them from

Fig. 6   Christian bronze lamp from Tiberias, now in the Case Archaeological Collection, University of Chicago. Fifth century

their pagan contemporaries. The time was still distant when the head of a Christian household and his wife who wished to live *comme il faut* should adorn themselves with rings, neck-laces and bracelets on which Christ and His Apostles were prominently displayed; should illuminate their houses with lamps decorated with the Chi-rho, use crystal table-ware with Christian fish engraved on it, and should even sanctify a water tap with large and uncompromising crosses.

By far the greatest part of the archaeological record is pre-served in the Roman Catacombs, originally named after the cemetery *ad catacumbas* along the Appian Way where, accord-ing to pious tradition, St Peter had been buried after his martyrdom. In the early days of the Church, Christians, Jews and pagans seem to have been buried side by side without discrimination of race or religion, and the integrity of all tombs was guaranteed under Roman law. Yet the Christians, as a unique and exclusive body, very soon adopted the idea of a community of the faithful that remained united even in death. Passionate believers in the resurrection of the body, the Christians, like the Jews, practised inhumation, and in the subterranean galleries excavated in the tufa beds just outside Rome they had ample room for the burial of their dead. At Naples, Syracuse and elsewhere there were other catacombs, but by far the most important were those near Rome. The earliest interments, and with them their associated wall paint-ings and epitaphs, seem to belong to the end of the second

Fig. 7   Gold pendant cross with five red stones. Height, 1¼ in.; width, 1 in. Walters Art Gallery, Balti-more.   Early   sixth century

Fig.   8   Gold   and amethyst ear-ring. Height, 3¾ in. Walters Art Gallery, Balti-more. Sixth century

81

century, and constitute the only considerable body of evidence for the art of the primitive Church. The Catacombs continued to be used into the fifth century, but even before then their importance was declining, as the Church emerged from the shadows into the daylight, and Christians provided their dead with more elaborate and costlier memorials.

So much has been preserved at Rome and so very little else-where that the role of the capital in the history of early Christian art, as opposed to the other great centres of the Christian world, stands in danger of being over-estimated. The apparent pre-eminence of Rome is, in fact, due to the existence and position of the Catacombs, which have given to the epitaphs and frescoes in them a unique chance of survival. In the Near East, which was certainly as profitable a field as Rome for the Church's earliest missions, the record is tantalizingly small, not least perhaps because the cities of Constantinople, Antioch, Jerusalem and Alexandria have all been lost to Christendom. Epigraphy forms a remarkable exception, and over the past century inscriptions have thrown considerable light on the condition of the Christian population there. Further excavation may produce more positive evidence, but until it is available the overall picture will necessarily be one-sided.

At the start, as a result of historical and geographical factors, the traditions of sculpture and painting in Rome itself, in the provinces and in the lands outside the imperial frontiers were extraordinarily diverse; thus a new iconography was practically the only common factor in all Christian artistic endeavour. In the analysis of the art of the early Church that follows, this new iconography will be discussed, and an attempt made to evaluate the importance and influence of different areas with recognizable stylistic conventions. However, in speaking of the earliest Christian art it is well to remember that 'art' is here a relative term, for much of it is pretty incompetent, distinguished more for its pious intent than for its successful execution. Such as it was, however, it was normally expressed in the language of symbolism, much of it freely borrowed from paganism. (From the first, the Church made sure that the Devil should not have a monopoly of all the good tunes!) Scenes from the Old Testament which prefigure the message of Christ are found in the late second and third centuries; so too, though more rarely, are incidents from the New Testament. The frescoes at Dura record scenes from both.

Fig. 9   Earliest known representation of the Crucifixion; graffito on the wall of a house on the Palatine in Rome. Christ is blasphemously shown with an ass's head

The death of Christ 'who his own self bare our sins in his own body on the tree, that we, being dead to sins, should live unto righteousness' was, together with the Resurrection, the corner-stone of the whole Christian edifice, then as now. Yet, the first known representation of the Crucifixion is a blasphemy, an almost illiterate scribble on the wall of a house on the Palatine hill in Rome. It depicts an ass crucified, with a man standing close by, his arms raised in prayer. Below, the con-temptuous legend reads: 'Alexamenos worships God.' The

Fig. 9

83

Greek name suggests that its owner was probably a slave, now become the butt of his fellow servants for his belief in Christ. To the Christian, the Crucifixion was the supreme act of redemption; but to the world at large the cross, like the modern gallows, was a symbol of shame until Constantine abolished that form of execution in 315. 'I offer my life's breath', says St Ignatius of Antioch to the Ephesians, 'for the sake of the cross, which is a scandal [i.e. a stumbling block] to the unbelievers, but to us it is salvation and eternal life.' Yet the cross itself, now identified with Christian art for more than sixteen centuries, was, when it was used at all, generally disguised. There are, of course, notable exceptions, and in a recently discovered cemetery near Jerusalem, which is un/ doubtedly earlier than the destruction of the city by Titus in 70, some of the ossuaries were found to be signed with a cross, either incised or marked with charcoal. If indeed these are the burials of Christians, as is just possible (though not perhaps very likely), they are the earliest material evidence of the Church's existence in Jerusalem or anywhere else.

Even in the Catacombs the symbol is rare before the Peace of the Church, and where it does exist, it lacks the note of challenge that still sounds across the centuries in the epitaphs of the Montanist heretics of Asia Minor. This sect, which came into being in the second half of the second century, believed in a new revelation of the Holy Spirit through the mouths of their prophets Montanus, Maximilla and Priscilla, and in the imminent appearance of a new Jerusalem at the little town of Pepuza in Phrygia. Ignoring the Church's ruling to Christians to bide their time and avoid provocation, they defiantly pro/ claimed their faith in a new and challenging formula, 'Christians to Christians', and by their open use of the upright cross either as a symbol on its own or as a substitute for the Greek letter *chi*, the initial letter of Christ's name. Moreover,

Fig. 10 Montanist inscription from the valley of the river Tembris in Phrygia. The eighth letter of the fourth line and the ninth letter of the fifth are upright crosses, replacing the usual form of the letter chi in the formula Χριστιανοὶ Χριστιανοῖς. Third century

these stones were set up not in secret, but in surface cemeteries to be seen by all.

Less inspiring perhaps to the modern eye, but surely equally so for the first Christians, are the symbols used partially to disguise the emblem of the cross. One of these is the tau-cross, the cross in the form of a capital 'T'. The Phrygian relief in Kütahya (see p. 66) seems to contain one in the bunch of grapes held in the extended left palm of the man who holds a quartered loaf in his right. The stem is quite simply suspended from a cross bar, and without further confirmation the evidence might seem too slight for serious consideration. On the other hand, from Phrygia in particular, are many examples of a fish or pair of fish suspended from a cross bar, often with apparently pagan motives on otherwise 'neutral' epitaphs. We cannot be sure that such stones are Christian, though they well may be. It is, in any case, certain that of the multitude of known pre-Constantinian grave-stones many more must have marked

Fig. 10

a

b

c

d

e

*Fig. 11   Some early
forms of the cross
symbol: (a) the tau-
cross, (b) the anchor,
(c) in scenes of
Jonah's misadventure
at sea; (d) and (e)
are both post-Con-
stantinian and based
on the chi-rho mono-
gram*

Christian burials than will ever be recognized from their content.

In the Western Church the anchor was commonly used as an alternative to the cross in the epitaphs of the third and early fourth centuries; it also symbolized Hope. Similarly, in the scene of Jonah's deliverance from the sea-monster, so often depicted in the Catacomb frescoes and on the earliest sculptured sarcophagi, the mast and yard of the prophet's ship, which combine to form a cross, are often prominent. In Egypt, the pagan symbol of life, the *ankh*, was near enough to a cross to be adopted by local Christians as a suitable emblem of their faith.

Second only to the cross as a symbol widely known to every generation of Christians is the fish, which is known to have been identified from the second century onwards with Christ Himself, and so, by a simple association of ideas, with the elements of the Eucharist and also with Baptism.

How this identification with Christ first arose is by no means certain, though it is easy to see why, once established, it became so popular. The fish could in fact bear a number of interpreta-tions, even though it was not, like the cross, a symbol embrac-ing in itself alone the whole significance of the Christian religion. It was Robert Mowat, an epigraphist, who first suggested that the fish might be a cryptogram, adopted by the Christians because in Greek the word *IXΘΥΣ* (fish) provides the initial letters of the profession of faith Ἰησοῦς Χριστὸς Θεοῦ Υἱὸς Σωτήρ—Jesus Christ, Son of God and Saviour. This interpretation has been almost universally accepted, and Tertullian seems to use the word in just this sense when he writes, 'We little fish, like our Ichthys Jesus Christ, are born of water'. The theory is attractive and must surely be correct, but it is unlikely that a cryptogram, however apt and charming, would have made so strong an impact all over the Christian world unless the fish had itself some particular significance.

To begin with the obvious, the symbol provides a link with

Fig. 12 Epitaph in the Museo Cristiano Vaticano, with two fish facing each other across an anchor, symbol of the cross, and so of Salvation. Above them is the legend 'The Fish of the Living.' Third century

two of Our Lord's major miracles, the Feeding of the Five Thousand and the Miraculous Draught. It also inevitably recalls His words to SS Peter and Andrew, 'Follow me and I will make you fishers of men'. This idea clearly underlies the third-century mosaic scene of a fisherman and his catch on a wall of the Tomb of the Julii in the Vatican Cemetery, and the theme was elaborated in the famous floor mosaic at Aquileia (314–320).

Confirmation of the way in which the symbol was identified with Communion is to be found in the Monument of Avircius, where the bishop tells how his brethren 'gave me to eat every-where the pure Fish of great size from the fountain'. In another important epitaph from Autun (probably a fifth- or sixth-century copy of a pre-Constantinian original), the dead man, Pectorius, addresses his fellow Christians as 'Celestial race of the Divine Fish', and continues, 'Eat with joy, holding the Fish in your hands', in this way referring to the manner in which the Host was then, and later, received: as, for example, in the illustration depicting the Communion of the Apostles in the sixth-century Rossano Codex. The appearance of the fish with bread and wine in some of the Catacomb frescoes is of rather more dubious interpretation. Possibly it symbolizes

87

the presence of Christ in the sacred elements; on the other hand, it may be no more than part of the food and drink taken by companies of Christians who gathered at tombs to celebrate with a *refrigerium* the anniversaries of the faithful. Fish, especially a large fish, was a great delicacy at Rome, as Juvenal reminds us in his Fourth Satire, where Domitian holds a Cabinet meeting to decide on the disposal of a 'turbot of fantastic size' which a fisherman had presented to the Emperor.

Fig. 13   Gravestone in the Museo Cristiano Lateranense. The orans *with doves represents the soul in Paradise. Fourth century*

Christ and His miracles; the elements of Communion and the fare of a refreshment meal; Baptism and the universal mission of the Church—all these were symbolized by the fish. Where this notion of the Divine Fish originated, however, remains unexplained. In Syria, the goddess Atargatis was worshipped in the form of a fish, and some of her devotees used to eat a meal of fish (although this was normally forbidden) in the hope of assimilating some of the goddess's

powers. In Edessa (modern Urfa), pools of sacred carp still   Plate 7
survive near the Ibrahim Paşa Camii as an object of popular
superstition. No one is allowed to molest, let alone catch them,
and the fish are so numerous that many of them are bruised and
torn from constant jostling in the water. Was this reverence
for the fish in ancient Syria and Northern Mesopotamia trans/
ferred to the worship of Christ by His early followers? If so, the
invention of the Christian cryptogram to give an air of respecta/
bility to a fundamentally pagan subject is readily intelligible.

The dove, whether by itself or with a veiled female *orans*, is   Fig. 13
commonly used to symbolize the soul, and is found in frescoes
and sarcophagus reliefs, most commonly against a background
of trees and flowers in scenes representing the bliss of Paradise.
There is also sometimes a pastoral element, provided by the
young shepherd surrounded by his flock or carrying a lamb
across his shoulders in the, to us, familiar attitude of the Good
Shepherd.

Although it has long passed out of use among the laity, the
Roman attitude of prayer, with arms outstretched and the
hands held palm outwards and slightly raised, is still familiar
in the Roman rite, for example during the reading of the Gospel
and much of the Canon. It is a simple, dignified, and devo/
tional gesture, with something of awe in it too, and is found
commonly throughout early Christian art wherever the person
concerned is to be thought of in close communion with God.
Thus, Noah standing in the Ark, Susannah in the Garden or
the Three Children in the Fiery Furnace are shown in this
attitude, no less than the draped female personage who
represents the soul of the blessed in Paradise. Of this latter,
one of the most beautiful examples is a young girl, against a   Plate 12
background of fruit trees in blossom, with a bird flying towards
her. It was painted in the Catacomb of Callixtus, probably not
long before the Peace of the Church. A few decades earlier,
in the centre of the famous sarcophagus in S. Maria Antiqua,

Plate 14

she appears flanked by trees and with the bird this time at her feet. Not far away, on her left, is the figure of the Good Shepherd, a lamb across His shoulders.

One of the commonest of Christian symbolic subjects before Constantine, the Good Shepherd is less frequently found in later Church art. A possible explanation of this may be that, while it had obvious associations with Christ's words in St John x, 14, it could be considered as iconographically neutral so far as the Christians' pagan neighbours were concerned and so was not a source of danger in time of persecution. Statues of Hermes Criophorus or of a simple worshipper carrying an animal to the sacrifice were common enough in Classical sculpture from the sixth century B.C. onwards, and a statue or picture of the Good Shepherd need have caused no eyebrow raising. It was, incidentally, one of the few subjects chosen by Christians for sculpture in the round—the beautiful marble statuette in Rome of Christ the Teacher is otherwise unknown—and so many of these statues have survived that it is interesting to speculate for what purpose they were made. Very possibly the figure would have been set up in the houses of Christians, or even of religious pagans who, like Alexander Severus, respected Christ without accepting his exclusive Divinity. It is also likely that it was part of the furniture of early churches both before and after Constantine, and it is noteworthy that a painting of Christ the Good Shepherd appears above the font in the Baptistery at

Plate 13

Dura. Of the statues, a famous example in the Lateran Museum is undoubtedly the finest. Until fairly recently it used to be dated far too early, even to the second century, but it is nowadays generally agreed to be a work of the late third or early fourth. Christ is depicted as a young, unbearded figure (the universal type of Christ in the early Church), holding a sheep with both hands across His shoulders. It is an old subject treated in a highly original manner. In many contemporary and later examples of such statues, little or no attempt is made to express the emotional link between the Shepherd and His charge. In the Lateran statue, however, the expression of the young Shepherd is gently concerned, while the sheep strains away from Him as if to avoid His attention.

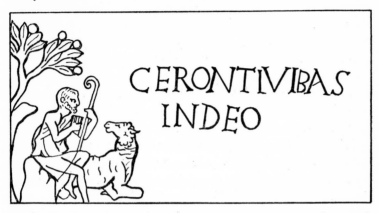

Fig. 14   Pre-Constantinian epitaph in the Museo Cristiano Lateranense with a pastoral scene. The inscription reads 'Gerontius, mayest thou live in God'. Late third century

Frescoes of the Good Shepherd often recall the words of Avircius Marcellus, who described himself as 'disciple of a pure shepherd with all-seeing eyes, who feeds his flocks on mountains and in the plains'. The simple bucolic scene was popular in late Classical art, and many of the representations of the Good Shepherd have a 'picturesque' background, of the type sometimes associated with the school of Alexandria. Such a background, by a natural transference of associations, became the Christian Paradise, where Christ was to be seen in the company of the elect, normally in the *orans* posture, or surrounded by His flock. Thus He appears in the Dura painting, and again in a fresco from the Catacomb of Domitilla. The same tradition too lies behind the magnificent fifth-century mosaic in the western lunette of the Mausoleum of Galla Placidia at Ravenna, where the subject appears for the last

Plate 68

Plate 9

time in early Christian art. A third-century painting in the Catacomb of Callixtus is less elaborate, and closer in feeling to the Lateran statuette. There is still, however, a sketchy background of trees, against which the young Shepherd stands between two lambs, with a third secured by His left hand over His shoulders. In His right He carries a metal cauldron for cooking a simple meal in the open air. The Shepherd also appears sometimes on gravestones as a symbol of Christianity, *Fig. 14* as, for example, in the third century epitaph of Gerontius.

Another allegorical figure also found in pastoral scenes, and especially on sculptured sarcophagi (e.g. in S. Maria Antiqua *Plates 14, 35* and another in the Lateran Museum), is the seated philosopher with his roll. Originally he symbolized the follower of Christ's true philosophy, but later became a stock type for the Evangelists in Church iconography throughout the Christian world, from the Byzantine mosaics of S. Vitale in Ravenna to the Hiberno-Northumbrian art of the Lindisfarne Gospels (*c.* 700), and even later to the eclectic school of the Carolingian period.

In all cases where its myths could be suitably converted to Christian use, Paganism made a direct contribution, for it was hardly to be expected that peoples long accustomed to religious art should be prepared to forego their entire heritage. It is true that some of the Fathers looked askance at every manifestation of paganism, and Clement of Alexandria early in the third century was at pains to warn his flock that only certain subjects could be countenanced by the devout Christian, and that they should at all costs avoid idolatry. Religious art is, however, not at all the same thing as idolatry. Moreover, the taste of the people and—perhaps even more important—the limited repertory of artists and craftsmen working for pagan as well as Christian patrons, ensured the survival of several pagan symbols and myths, which attained in official Church iconography complete respectability. Even Dante chose as his guide through the Underworld the well-loved pagan Virgil, who had 'foretold' the coming of Christ in his Fourth Eclogue.

The vintage feast, characteristic of Dionysiac funerary art, and as we see it in the ambulatory mosaics of S. Costanza in Rome, could easily be given a Christian significance. Even when the *amores* disappeared from the scene, the vine scroll remained as a permanent feature of Church symbolism. Orpheus, who drew all living creatures to himself by his music, was also converted. Most striking of all perhaps is the mosaic in the vault of the Tomb of the Julii in the Vatican Cemetery, where Christ is depicted as the Sun of Righteousness in his Chariot. In the field of symbolism, the peacock with its incorruptible flesh became a type of Immortality. Victories attendant upon the divine Emperor became angels, ministers of Christ triumphant. The victorious athlete's palm signified the eternal reward of those who had died, especially of martyrs. Even the cornucopia survived, as a reminder perhaps that 'of His fulness we have all received'.

Under the later Empire even the Jews were prepared to tolerate representational art. In the Dura synagogue, Abraham may be seen receiving the covenant, and the vision of Ezekiel in the Valley of Dry Bones is presented as a dramatic tableau, with the presence of God the Father indicated—as so often in contemporary Christian art—by a hand reaching out of heaven. On a fragmentary sarcophagus (*c.* 300) in Rome, pagan *amores*, one of them holding a cornucopia, disport themselves on either side of the seven-branched candlestick. Even more significant, however, is the fact that Old Testament scenes, as they are represented in both painting and sculpture, display a maturity and consistency of iconography that is only consonant with a long and established tradition. It has been argued, particularly by Professor Talbot Rice, that this iconography probably reflects the original illustrations of the Alexandrian Septuagint. Considering the importance of

Plate 21

Plates 27, 29

Alexandria as an artistic centre in the first centuries of our era, and the picturesque element in many of the Old Testament subjects treated, such an explanation, although in the nature of things unprovable, seems not at all unlikely. The iconography connected with the New Testament is also surprisingly con﹀ sistent from the earliest times, though there are few definite clues to an ultimate source. Naturally enough the individual subjects in both the Old and New Testaments were variously treated according to the prevailing canons of artistic taste in different periods and localities, but by and large, and allowing for inevitable exceptions, there seems to have been a parallel development in East and West so far as the arrangement of subject matter was concerned.

The episodes from the Old Testament most commonly found in the earliest Christian art are those that best symbolize the theme of the Redemption. In times of persecution too, the trials of Daniel in the Lions' Den, of Jonah in the belly of the whale or of the Three Children in the Fiery Furnace were specially apt, and appear early in Patristic literature (e.g. Clement, Cor. 45). 'Lord, deliver us from the lion's maw' was a prayer often only too apposite in its literal sense. The tale of Susanna and the Elders, also connected with Daniel, was another theme specially popular with early iconographers, and was perhaps intended as a model for Christian womanhood.

In many of the early Catacomb paintings, these stories are illustrated in the simplest manner. In the Catacomb of
Plate 10
Priscilla, the Three Children in their clothes of Lincoln green stand immobile, arms raised in prayer, while sketchy flames lick their feet. In the so﹀called *capella greca* of the same Cata﹀ comb, the paintings are still more severe. Moses striking the living water from the rock (a subject based on I Cor. x, 4, and one of the commonest in early Christian art) makes no claim to naturalistic treatment, while Susanna (in the *orans* posture) between Daniel and the two Elders is all that remains of the

lurid account of the Apocrypha. On the sarcophagus of Velletri (*c.* 300) even the story of Noah is reduced to a praying figure who stands upright in his diminutive box-like ark. All dramatic possibilities seem to have been deliberately ignored, perhaps because the artist would have dismissed too much picturesque detail in strictly biblical scenes as irrelevant, or even as meretricious. Pure incompetence was also certainly a con-tributory factor in many cases. This judgment is borne out by the fact that early Christian sarcophagi are normally of far higher quality. These would have been manufactured by professionals working regularly for pagan as well as Christian clients, while the choice of painters to work in the Catacombs would before Constantine have been limited to members of the Christian community. (The obviously poor quality of the Velletri sarcophagus does not invalidate this proposition. To judge from his familiarity with biblical subjects—the miracle of the Multiplication of the Loaves and Fishes is included—the maker was almost certainly a Christian, while the harsh carving and inadequacy of arrangement stamps the work as that of a third-rate mason.)

The Jonah trilogy demanded more elaborate treatment, and lent itself specially well to the episodic technique of historical relief which, although originally a Hellenistic invention, was only fully developed in the Roman period. The sequence of events, whether on sarcophagi or in Catacomb paintings, is well-nigh invariable. Jonah is first seen being hurled head first from the ship into the jaws of the great fish, which usually appears in the form of the Classical *ketos*—a sort of bearded sea-serpent with ears. The prophet is next disgorged on dry land, while in the final scene he rests beneath the shade of the gourd-tree. In pre-Constantinian times the story was de-servedly popular as a symbol of the Christian's triumph over death and his later enjoyment of the heavenly *refrigerium* in Paradise. On sarcophagi of the earlier period, the scene is best

Plate 15

treated in the example from S. Maria Antiqua and is in direct descent from the Hellenistic tradition. Cruder are those of the sarcophagi of Velletri and of Baebia Hermophile in Rome (see p. 99). A third-century painting in the Catacomb of Callixtus makes the most of a dramatic situation, with the monster seen first waiting expectantly for his victim and then, turned about, striking out strongly for the shore and the gourd covered bower where Jonah is to rest after his experience. Jonah also figures on a wall mosaic in the Tomb of the Julii in Rome, but here is depicted, unusually, being engulfed feet first.

Scenes that are strictly Christian, as opposed to those derived from the Old Testament alone, may be divided into two categories. There are those which illustrate events in the Gospels (which include episodes in the life of Our Lord and some of His miracles), and those which concern the life of the Early Church in the Sacraments of Baptism and the Eucharist.

The Infant Christ in the arms of His mother forms the theme of two very different paintings, both in the Catacomb of Priscilla. The first represents the fulfilment of the prophecy of Isaiah (VII, 14)—'Behold a virgin shall conceive, and shall bear a son, and shall call his name Immanuel'. It is one of the most beautiful of all early Christian paintings, and cannot be dated on stylistic grounds any later than the beginning of the third century. To the left stands Isaiah, while the Virgin is shown with the Infant struggling at her breast and turning His face away from her; a star shines above them. The treatment is in the late Hellenistic impressionist manner, but the subject is new. Towards the end of the same century, the scene was repeated, this time as a simple group of mother and child. (The *orans* to the left is not relevant to the composition. Unlike the earlier picture, the style of this one is severe, tending already towards the fully 'expressionist' treatment of the famous Madonna and Child in the Coemeterium Maius (see p. 159).) The Adoration

Plate 16

of the Magi (in the same Catacomb) is also found very early, as a symbol of the universality of the Kingship of Christ and of His Church. The iconography of this scene, with the Three Kings advancing one behind the other on bended knee towards the Virgin and Child, remains consistent over the centuries.

Most events in the life of Christ which were used as subjects for painting and sculpture before the Peace of the Church are, like their Old Testament counterparts, those which illustrate the Deliverance of Mankind. The sacrifice of the Cross itself was in a sense almost too topical, too controversial a subject to be commemorated in the visual arts. Consequent on this early neglect, the treatment of the Crucifixion never achieved until much later the same stability of iconography as did other subjects which had been used from the first. The Resurrection and the Ascension are likewise not seen until after Constantine, unless the rather enigmatic scene on the northern wall of the Dura Baptistery is to be interpreted as the three Marys arriving at the Sepulchre on the the first Easter morning.

Plate 2

Christ's meeting with the woman of Samaria at the well, His healing of the paralytic and rescue of St Peter from sinking into the Sea of Galilee are all portrayed in the Dura Baptistery. The style is simple to the point of naïveté; nor had the painter any sense of composition, and on the northern wall, above the 'three Marys', the two miracles are shown side by side without so much as a dividing line between them. In Rome, where two of these scenes—the woman at the well and the healing of the paralytic—are to be found before the end of the third century in the Catacomb of Callixtus, the style is more sophisticated, yet the essential treatment of the events is the same. The woman is shown in the act of lowering her bucket into the water, while the paralytic stoops under the load of his stretcher bed. Even in the scene on Lake Tiberias, the broad face of St Peter with the curly hair and beard that are so familiar

97

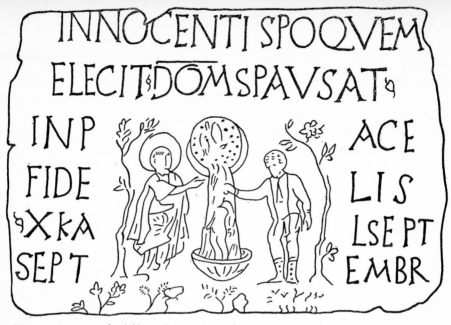

INNOCENTI SPOQVEM
ELECIT§DOMSPAVSAT˦
INP ACE
FIDE LIS
˦XKA LSEPT
SEPT EMBR

Fig. 15   Gravestone of a child named Innocentius in the Museum at Aquileia. The scene represents his baptism by the Holy Spirit in the form of a dove, in the circular aura above his head. To his right and left are a saint and a priest. Fourth-fifth century

in later Christian art are recognizable. Such similarities can hardly be accidental, and combine to suggest strongly an Oriental provenance for the iconography of the New Testa-ment, and although there is no western example comparable in date with the Dura paintings, the usual treatment of the Adoration of the Magi, with the Kings advancing in line (cf. the 'three Marys'), seems to be in the same tradition. If so, there is a clear divergence of origins as between New and Old Testament iconography, as the latter, in Christian hands, owes nothing to the Synagogue artist at Dura, but apparently a great deal to a Hellenistic source.

Other miracles of Our Lord occur rarely. On the Velletri sarcophagus, the Multiplication is depicted with Christ holding two crossed loaves in His raised hands, the usual seven baskets of fragments standing before Him. The healing of the woman with the issue of blood appears on a fragmentary sarcophagus relief in Rome, in a form very close to the type which became canonical in the post-Constantinian period. In the Catacomb of Callixtus, Christ is seen raising Lazarus from the dead.

The New Testament scenes at Dura were all specially appropriate to the catechumen approaching Baptism. Christ's conversation with the Samaritan woman emphasized the power of the Living Water to ensure eternal life, while the two miracles pointed the necessity for faith in overcoming adversity and evil. No picture of Christ's Baptism has survived at Dura, but it is hard to believe that none existed among the many paintings which we know to have been lost; all the more so, because baptismal scenes, with an apparently established iconography, are met with as early as the third century in the Catacomb of Callixtus and on the S. Maria Antiqua sarco-phagus. These are extremely simple, containing only two figures, with a dove, personifying the Holy Spirit, hovering above. Whether in these cases the allusion is specifically to Our Lord's Baptism or to the Sacrament in general is not clear, though the youth of the baptized person in the sarcophagus relief rather suggests the latter. The fourth-century baptismal scene inscribed on a gravestone in Aquileia is certainly generalized.

Plate 14

Fig. 15

The institution of the Eucharist is never directly represented in pre-Constantinian art, though it appears time and again under the symbol of the refreshment meal (*refrigerium*) at which the elements of bread and wine are always present, and some-times the fish also. The number at table is usually seven, and on either side, or in front of it, are often ranged the same number of baskets, in an obvious reference to the miracle of the Multiplication. The rendering of the scene varies chiefly in atmosphere, from the near-pagan roystering on the sarcophagus relief of Baebia Hermophile in Rome to the devotional painting in the *capella greca* of the Catacomb of Priscilla, which has

Plate 8

actually been claimed as representing the Eucharistic breaking of bread (*fractio*) itself. Both this, and another more pedestrian work in the Catacomb of Callixtus include the fish as part of the fare, though it is absent from both the sarcophagus of Baebia Hermophile and also from a broken relief of the same subject in Rome. It is the fish, symbol of Christ, which gives point to the paintings; indeed, it is enough, with the bread and wine, to symbolize the Eucharistic meal without any further concession to realism in the form of human participants. In the Crypts of Lucina (Catacomb of Callixtus), the living fish beside a basket containing a cup of wine and covered by a plate of loaves may be considered a Christian *refrigerium* in shorthand

Fig. 12 —more, it is the Eucharist itself. The Fish of the Living, inscribed on an epitaph in the Vatican Museum, can only symbolize Christ; thus associated with bread and wine, the meaning of the picture is clear beyond reasonable doubt. Why the fish is missing from the sarcophagus reliefs is not clear. Perhaps the sculptors were commissioned to execute *refrigeria* scenes, quite simply, without any Christian overtones. This might also explain why the number at table is five in one case

Plates 6, 8 and only three in the other, instead of the significant seven. However this may be, when in the fourth century the Euchar‑ istic scene gained immeasurably in authority from the dominant presence of Christ at the gathering, its origin was still demon‑ strably firmly rooted in pre‑Constantinian renderings of symbolic *refrigeria*.

Contrasted with the wealth of subjects available to, and employed by, artists after the Peace of the Church, the repertory of the earlier Christians appears limited indeed, and almost as if it were the result of a random selection. While granting that a free choice of subjects was often unfavourably influenced, in the Empire at any rate, by the political situation, three facts should be borne in mind, of which the first, the scantiness of the archaeological record for the earliest centuries, is the most important. With Dura, the Catacombs and scattered epi-graphic finds all that remain as positive evidence, we are not even in a position to assess the probable extent of our losses, particularly in the eastern territories of Christendom. To consider an isolated instance, David and Goliath appear in the church at Dura, but nowhere else, so far as our record goes. It is inherently unlikely that the scene was exclusive to Dura; and if that is true of one subject, how can we be certain that others have not temporarily disappeared in the same way? The second fact is that the survival of post-Constantinian churches with their decoration, and of other monuments and *objets d'art* is due to conditions exactly the opposite of those with which the first Christians had to contend. Finally, the 'new' subjects current in the fourth and fifth centuries do not appear one after the other with a slowly developing iconography. On the con-trary, the majority appear simultaneously, and with a consistency of iconography that suggests an earlier period of development from a recognized prototype. In the case of the Old Testament, we may suppose the influence of the Septuagint illustrations, while if Dura holds a clue to the provenance of New Testament iconography, the East may well have some surprises in store.

The art of the early Church was inevitably a product of its own age, since although the Christian message was new and without precedent, it could only be expressed through the same media and conventions that governed contemporary art in the different lands to which it so soon spread. It is, for that reason, fortunate that if the larger part of the record was fated to be preserved in a single city, that city should have been a cosmo-politan city like Rome, which was a common meeting-ground for different schools with varying artistic traditions.

Attempts are often made to classify individual works of the early Christian period according to the known, or supposed characteristics of different schools which influenced art at Rome during the first three centuries after Christ, and in some cases

Plates 10, 12

Plate 16

such a classification is quite possible and profitable. It is plain, for example, that the paintings of the *Orans* in the Catacomb of Priscilla and of the Three Children in the Catacomb of Callixtus are governed by different artistic conventions; it is plain too that neither has anything in common with the Madonna and Child in the Coemeterium Maius. However, these are all works of some merit and character, and there are many others, equally interesting historically, which cannot be categorized at all, any more than could be the contents of a monumental mason's atelier today. If, in these undistinguished examples of early Christian art, there is a tendency towards 'expressionism', to the rejection of refinement or picturesque detail, it may be explained not so much as due to the infiltration of ideas from Asia Minor and Syria—though these may have had their influence—as to a lack of interest in a painting or relief except as the vehicle for a message. The sarcophagus of Velletri is a good case in point.

Where pagan art is concerned, the issue is usually clearer, and various labels have been introduced to distinguish between this or that school. Recently, by general usage, the terms 'Neo-Attic' and 'Alexandrian' have gained currency as descriptive of the two main streams of Hellenistic art during the first two centuries before and after Christ.

Neo-Attic, an almost self-explanatory term, describes that branch of Hellenistic art which most closely followed the earlier Hellenic tradition, whereby the elements of time and space were eliminated in favour of a generalized approach to the subject. The Panathenaic procession represented in the frieze of the Parthenon is not limited in space by a specific background or in time by the intrusion of a specific occasion. Similarly, the human figure, although expressed with realism, is independent of any artifice aimed at producing an illusion-istic effect. A Greek vase-painting of the early fifth century B.C. epitomizes the Classical style even more accurately. The curved surface of the pot militates against illusionism in any form, while the red-figure technique (whereby figures are reserved in the red colour of the clay against a background of shiny black) effectively limits the picture to two dimensions. This kind of painting declined, inevitably, from the moment that artists tried to follow the masters of 'free' painting into a third dimension. As for sculpture, when Hellenism became diluted as it spread into Asia and Egypt, much of the old discipline was lost, though its outward form survived on the Greek mainland, in coastal Asia Minor, and in Italy. In Rome, the frieze of the Ara Pacis Augustae with its slow, dignified procession of the Imperial family and the Roman people is, although vitiated by a sense of occasion, in conscious descent from the Hellenic tradition; so too is the art of the Hadrianic period. This academic, sometimes almost arid style seems to have appealed to the conservatism of the more cultured classes of Imperial Rome, but before the fall of paganism it found little favour in the Christian art of the capital, though the Lateran Good Shepherd forms an obvious exception. In the East, on the other hand, it held its own, for its austere discipline was more in tune with Oriental tradition than the picturesque style that was making headway elsewhere in the Christian world. Certainly the Neo-Attic school played an important role in the formation of the art of the First Golden Age of Byzantium, as is clear from the two famous mosaic panels of Justinian and Theodora in the church of S. Vitale in Ravenna.

Plate 13

Plate 78

'Alexandrian', as descriptive of the other main school of Hellenistic art, of course begs the question of ultimate provenance, since from Alexandria itself there is little material evidence to confirm that the style originated there. Literary sources and the fact that Egyptian features and Nilotic scenes are often prominent in 'Alexandrian' art, seem to justify the use of the adjective in connexion with an impressionistic style, in which landscape of a fantastic and sometimes almost dreamlike quality acts as background to the activities of the human characters. Of this style the panoramic scenes from the Odyssey in the House of Livia in Rome are typical. It may be, as C. R. Morey suggested, that the 'Alexandrian' style represents a progressive school of art that arose in the newer centres of Hellenism (e.g. Alexandria and Antioch), established by Alexander and his successors. In any case it had spread to Italy by the first century B.C., and at Pompeii, in many of the paintings that were based on Hellenistic originals, there is an intrusive picturesque element. This 'Alexandrian' style played an important role in the development of early Christian art, for much of which it was specially suitable. The bliss of Paradise almost demanded a picturesque background of trees and birds

Plate 12

(e.g. the *Orans* in the Catacomb of Priscilla), and the Jonah trilogy also was the better for an appropriate setting. The style was not confined to painting, and appears to a marked degree in several pre-Constantinian sarcophagus reliefs. In the Good

Plate 35

Shepherd sarcophagus in the Lateran, only the central group is provided with a background of trees and sheep, but in S.

Plate 14

Maria Antiqua, although each figure, group or scene is not strictly speaking connected with its neighbour, an over-all unity is achieved by trees arranged like pictorial marks of punctuation. Details appropriate to individual scenes (e.g. water and a dove in the Baptism) are added where needed to lend emphasis.

The paintings in the synagogue and church at Dura represent a style which, owing almost nothing to Hellenism, was to have a great impact on early Christian art. The style was fore-shadowed in the wall paintings of yet another important building at Dura, the Temple of the Palmyrene Gods, which dates from the last quarter of the first century A.D. The picture known as the Sacrifice of Conon shows Conon himself and two white-robed priests wearing tall, conical hats, standing

Plate 2

side by side and facing the spectator (cf. the three 'Marys' in the church), against an architectural background. The treatment

of the drapery and its folds alone recall the art of the Mediter׳
ranean; otherwise the painting puts the viewer, almost literally,
face to face with the Orient. No illusion of a third dimension
is either intended or achieved, and the figures in their frontal,
'hieratic' pose, are less aware of each other than they are of the
spectator. Thus, by a deliberate rejection of charm and
delicacy and the choice of an almost violent approach, the
artist allows his picture to speak directly for itself, with an
appeal less to the mind than to the emotions.

This style, currently known as 'expressionist', is primitive in
more than one sense of the word. It is certainly simpler than the
representational, if only because it requires less technical
expertise to produce an effect, though this is not to deny that
'expressionist' artists made a free choice between the two. That
they did so is quite clear from the growing popularity of the
'expressionist' style in Rome during the fourth century, where
the Hellenistic tradition was by no means yet dead. The origins
of the principle of frontality, the hallmark of the style, as
exemplified by the figures in the Sacrifice of Conon, may be
traced back in Western Persia to the eighth century B.C. in the
bronzes of Luristan. Frontality is also the rule in Parthian and,
later, in Sassanian art, and it was through contact with neigh׳
bouring countries to the east that the Dura style certainly
developed.

Palmyra, on the other hand, closer to the Hellenistic fringe
of the Levant, became the home of a school of sculpture which
combined a certain taste for realism with a highly individual
and elaborate treatment of subject. Like the city of its origin,
Palmyrene art is an oasis, and no trace of its influence survives
in the sculpture or paintings of the early Church. Nevertheless,
from the Wadi el Miyah, not far eastward of Palmyra, comes
an extraordinary relief (now at Damascus) of a group of gods
standing side by side, where the style represents a real half׳way
house between the art of Hellenism and Dura. All the figures

conform to the law of frontality, yet the drapery is handled in the Classical manner.

The contribution of Asia Minor to the development of the 'expressionist' style is problematic, largely owing to a lack of monuments. It is true that sculpture in the round from some of the Syro-Hittite sites in the south-east (e.g. Carchemish, Malatya and Karatepe) is in the frontal manner, but equally so most of the relief sculpture is not. In any case the evidence is hard to evaluate, since the art, such as it is, is highly eclectic. More suggestive perhaps is the fact that all 'native' relief sculpture of the Hellenistic, Roman and early Christian periods observes the law of frontality, though normally (e.g. *Fig. 2* the Kütahya grave relief) the work is not distinguished enough to be dignified by the word 'expressionist'. It is probably premature to posit an Anatolian tradition in this matter, but it may be significant that an Anatolian *style* certainly existed in *Plates 46, 47, 48* early Christian art in the fifth century (e.g. the Adana reliquary *Fig. 31* and the sculptures of Alahan) and that this may be described as 'expressionist'. Whatever its antecedents, it was to form a most important ingredient in the fully developed art of Byzantium.

In early Christian Rome, all schools that have been described were represented, though the expressionist style only came into its own in the fourth century, in such a work as that of the *Plate 16* Madonna and Child in the Coemeterium Maius. Of a native Roman school that persisted through all the changes of artistic fashion, it is rather difficult to say anything positive, unless one is prepared to accept art in Rome as Roman art. A certain factual approach and an interest in narrative perhaps provide clues to its recognition, though these are more evident in post- rather than pre-Constantinian art, e.g. the Battle of the Milvian Bridge from the Arch of Constantine, and the mosaic scenes *Plates 72, 73* of the life of Our Lord from the top register of S. Apollinare Nuovo in Ravenna. However, many of the Catacomb painters will have been Romans, and their style may perhaps be discerned in the 'raw material' of Christian iconography in the Catacomb of Callixtus for example.

Professor Swift, in his *Roman Origins of Christian Art*, goes far towards denying a significant Eastern contribution. Before his time, Josef Strzygowski stated in his *Origins of Christian Church Art* that Hellenism had 'died in the embraces of the Orient'. The true answer surely lies somewhere between these two extreme points of view, and, in the words of Sir William Ramsay 'there is no religion but Christianity which is so wholly penetrated both with the European and with the Asiatic spirit —so penetrated that many are sensitive only to one or the other'.

CHAPTER IV

From Constantine to Justinian:
The Religious Background

THE BATTLE OF the Milvian Bridge had established
Constantine as the protector of the Christians, and the
following year, at Milan, Licinius became associated with him
in his new policy. Whether to the Christians recent events
would have seemed to herald the dawn of a new era is unlikely.
They certainly had good reason to be sceptical, for the older
men at least would have been able to remember Valerian's
persecution, and how the long peace that followed it had been
only the prelude to worse conditions under Diocletian and
Galerius. As it happened, they were not this time to be
deceived, for although Maximinus continued for some years to
harass the Christians of the East, and although Licinius later
turned persecutor on his own account, their champion Constantine never swerved in pursuit of his ambition to eliminate
all rivals and to become the sole ruler of the Roman world. In
323, Licinius, his last adversary, had been strangled, and
Constantine, who until then had granted the Christians parity
with their pagan fellows, now came out openly in their favour.
Since the death of his father, Constantius, seventeen years
before, Constantine had manipulated events to serve his own
ends. He had, literally and in his own person, made history;
now, as undisputed master of the Empire, it was in his power
to inaugurate a new era. This he did, both symbolically and in
fact, when on 11th May 330 he dedicated his new capital on
the shores of the Bosphorus.

The motives for his decision were political and religious.
The Tetrarchy was dead, and of the provincial cities of Trèves,

Milan, Sirmium and Nicomedia, which had served Diocletian and his colleagues well enough as headquarters, none was of sufficient status to be the administrative capital of a unified Empire, let alone of an Emperor like Constantine. Thus, the question of whether Rome could again fill this historic role was an urgent one. The old capital had an unrivalled prestige, but it also stood for the past, with which Constantine wished to break completely. It did not suit him to introduce new policies and a new religion in a city traditionally opposed to change, and whose most influential citizens were staunch supporters of the old pagan order. Furthermore, since Diocletian's day, the political centre of gravity had shifted eastwards, and the character of the principate itself had altered, to become some what akin to an Oriental despotism; the Christians too, from whom the Emperor drew his strongest support, were far more numerous in the eastern provinces than in the West. These considerations alone were enough to suggest a transference of the seat of government from Rome to the East; in fact, there were also good military reasons, and these probably influenced the Emperor's choice of site. Constantinople, at the point where Europe meets Asia, occupies a triangular promontory, defined to the north by the Golden Horn, to the south by the Sea of Marmara, and by its walls on the western, landward side. The city was thus exceptionally strong by nature, but in 330 there was another reason for its choice. The Empire was facing a double threat to its security, from the Sassanians on the eastern frontier, and from the Goths on the line of the Danube. An Emperor at Constantinople was far better placed to meet it than ever he could have been at Rome.

Constantinople on its seven hills, with its official Latin, its senate house, pagan temples and statues of the Emperors, was the new Rome; the same city, with its incomparable land and sea scapes over Europe and Asia, with its Greek speaking population, with its new churches built to the glory of the God of the Christians, was an eastern metropolis. Incongruous and incompatible though its constituent elements may nowadays seem, this hybrid character—as Constantine surely appreciated —was the very source of its original vitality. Indeed, more than a millennium after its foundation, when Constantinople had become almost entirely orientalized and the ties with Rome had been broken by the great schism of 954, Constantine XIII, the last of the Emperors, could still style himself 'King of the Romans'.

The years between the foundation of Constantinople and the accession of Justinian were crucial for the Church. In earlier times, the main issue was that of survival. With the establishment of Christianity as the State Religion, the Church's main concern was to defend orthodox dogma against the heresies that soon sprang up like so many mushrooms in the more favourable political climate. Apart from a brief neopagan interlude under Julian the Apostate (361–363), the Emperors were all Christian in name at least, and their supreme political power, coupled with the assumption of temporal authority in ecclesiastical matters, led them frequently to intervene in theological disputes. It was this intervention, with its consequent repercussions on relations between the Empire and the Papacy, that made the great heresies of the fourth and fifth centuries a matter of political, as well as of theological importance. During the preConstantinian period, the Church had dealt with the many heresies that arose—Gnostic, Montanist, Manichee and the rest—almost as a matter of family discipline, if only because the State neither understood nor cared about internal dissensions among Christians. When, unusually, an appeal was made to the Emperor in 273 in the case of Paul of Samosata, a deposed bishop, Aurelian gave judgment to the orthodox party to the dispute. With a Christian Emperor in Constantinople, and the Pope exercising a comparable, though different authority in the affairs of the

West, the new situation showed itself, as Diehl has so picturesquely put it concerning the period around the Council of Chalcedon (451), in the 'incongruity between the Oriental episcopate, docile to the will of the prince, and the unyielding and haughty intransigence of the Roman pontiffs'. It may seem curious to consider our period in terms of religious controversy, particularly in view of the momentous changes which took place in Europe, including the end of the Western Empire in 476, as a result of barbarian pressure and invasion. Nevertheless, the theological disputes were of greater importance in the history of the Church, and of these disputes the most violent were those caused by the heresies associated with Arius, Nestorius and Eutyches.

It is frequently thought that the theological arguments within the early Church and the disorders which they sometimes occasioned can be dismissed as a series of disgraceful squabbles over *minutiae*. Yet this is far from being the case. Rather, indeed the Church owes a great debt to those whose Faith was of such importance and a source of such enthusiasm that they were prepared to devote their lives to establishing it on a secure foundation. The heresies themselves were not entirely evil, since if the truth was to emerge dissension was well-nigh inevitable, and the tree has grown all the more healthily for its early pruning.

The essence of Arianism, first propounded in Alexandria, was the denial to God the Son of equality with God the Father, since Christ, though begotten of the Father before all ages, was yet a creature, in the sense that before Time began He had once not been. Also, by the Incarnation, Christ was susceptible to growth and physical change and to human emotions, and in this way too was not God's equal. The relation of the Holy Spirit to the Son was the same as that of Christ to the Father. This belief in a supreme God with two subordinates was directly opposed to orthodox Trinitarian dogma, and in

318, after complaints had been lodged against Arius, Alexander, patriarch of Alexandria, re-affirmed the orthodox position by declaring Christ to be of the same substance with the Father. This Arius rejected, and in 321 he was excom-municated by a synod of the bishops of Egypt and Libya. Arianism, however, continued to make ground, and the Emperor was asked to intervene. Reluctant at first, and dis-playing a contemptuous indifference to what he considered a waste of breath over trifles, Constantine finally decided to show his authority by convening an Oecumenical Council at Nicaea. There, in 325, the Nicene Creed was formulated and accepted by all except two of the delegates, and in it Christ was again defined as of the same substance with the Father.

With the death of Arius in 336 and of Constantine the following year, the dispute broke out with greater violence, and a confused situation was further confounded by the fact that of the three sons of the Emperor who succeeded him, Con-stantine II and Constans were orthodox churchmen who supported Nicaea, while Constantius II, who ruled the East and was destined to survive them both, was a convinced Arian. In the meanwhile, Athanasius, an inflexible opponent of Arianism at Nicaea, had succeeded his old friend and patron, Alexander, in the patriarchate of Alexandria. Sent into exile, Athanasius made his way to Rome, where his friendship with Pope Julius was instrumental for a time in the formation of a united orthodox front in a dispute that always threatened to divide on East–West lines. In 343, an attempt to reconcile growing differences was made at the Council of Sardica, but there was no agreement, and the Western bishops were alone in their support of Nicaea. The conflict dragged wearily on without an open breach until, with the death of Constans in 350 and the assassination of the usurper, Magnentius, three years later, the Roman world was once again governed by a single Emperor, Constantius II, the supporter of the Arians.

The heresy once established with official backing at once splintered. At Nicaea, Christ had been described as 'of the same substance' (*homo-ousios*) with the Father. The term was now successively altered, according to the tenets of whichever Arian sect happened to be influential, to 'unlike' (*anomoios*), 'of like substance' (*homoio-ousios*) and, finally, 'like' (*homoios*) to the Father. The confusions and contradictions were apparently limitless. Athanasius was again in exile, and his work seemed to have ended in failure. It took the accession of a pagan Emperor, Julian, to bring Christendom to its senses.

Julian, while proclaiming equality for all creeds, in fact tried to revive paganism. To this end he adopted many of the Christian values and details of Church organization, while discriminating against Christianity as such. He was a brilliant, if somewhat eccentric anachronism, but his pressure against all Christians, orthodox or heretical, naturally resulted in a closing of the ranks against him. Athanasius, recalled from exile in 362, the year before Julian was killed on the Persian front, now seized his opportunity, and at the Council of Alexandria won back to orthodoxy many of those Arians whose rejection of it had depended on a 'jot', the letter *iota* in *homoio-ousios* (of like substance), as against *homo-ousios* (of the same substance). After Julian's death, however, the Empire was again divided by the accession of Valentinian, a supporter of orthodoxy, in the West, and of Valens, an Arian, in the East. Fortunately for Christendom, there were now champions of Nicaea in both halves of the Empire; at Milan, Bishop Ambrose, outstanding theologian and hymn composer, stood firm behind Athanasius, while in the East, although Valens vigorously persecuted the orthodox, a new school of theology arose in Cappadocia, which was ultimately to bridge the gap between the opposing camps. The great names associated with this school are Basil of Caesarea, his brother Gregory of Nyssa, and Gregory Nazi-anzus. Basil, the founder of the coenobitic (communal) form of monasticism, was consecrated bishop of Caesarea in 370, three years before the death of Athanasius, and his work on the definition of the Trinitarian dogma in a see which controlled a large part of central Asia Minor, where the more moderate of the Arians were specially influential, was vitally important. In 378, Valens died, and in 381, in the reign of Theodosius I, the doctrine of the existence of Three Persons, Father, Son and Holy Ghost, in a Unity of Substance was accepted at the Council of Constantinople, and the whole controversy was settled in favour of orthodoxy by the re-affirmation of the Nicene Creed.

The conversion of Augustine, a Numidian by birth, who was later bishop of Hippo, took place in 386, five years after the condemnation of Arianism. Of all the Western Fathers none more than he was to influence the life of the Church in all its aspects. He spent most of his Christian life in combating heresy, and in doing so established a theological system which is still accepted, with reservations, today. He, above all, was the true founder of the Medieval Church in the West, which drew upon his many books and sermons not only for its theology, but also for its social and political ideology. His main efforts were directed against the Donatist and Pelagian heresies, though he also summarized the orthodox position *vis-à-vis* the Arians in his work *Concerning the Trinity*.

The Donatist schism, which began in Carthage early in the fourth century, arose in the aftermath of the great persecution, during which some of the clergy and laity of North Africa had come to terms with the persecutors, and so earned for themselves the name of 'traitors'. Amongst the suspects, Mensurius, the bishop of Carthage himself, stood accused by many of his flock, and on his death, his successor, Caecilianus, was equally unacceptable; the more so as one of the bishops present at his consecration was known to have been compliant during the persecution. In 313 a Numidian bishop, Donatus, appealed to the Emperor against the validity of Caecilianus' own consecration on these grounds, but the petition was rejected. However, in bringing forward the test case, the Donatists had also, by implication, called into question the validity of the sacraments when administered by an unworthy priest or bishop. For the Church to have accepted the Donatist position, that an act of apostasy or moral unworthiness could invalidate the powers of an ordained priest might easily have led to highly subjective judgments of what constituted apostasy, and the heresy was condemned at the Council of Carthage in 348. Trouble continued, however, and only came to an end at a second Council at Carthage in 411, when the doctrine of Augustine prevailed, viz. that any man, whatever his moral character, who had been ordained priest or consecrated bishop, was, by virtue of being Christ's intermediary, a valid minister of the sacraments. Validity depended, therefore, not on the character of the individual, but on his position as a representative of Christ.

As the military power of the Western Empire waned under the barbarian onslaughts, and as the Atlantic provinces in particular were increasingly less able to rely on Roman protection, so the Church in those lands gained in vitality and maturity. Britain, which for nearly four centuries had produced no outstanding churchman, now came to the fore, not it is true in the field of orthodoxy, but as the birthplace of Pelagius, a monk, whose heresies concerning original sin and the doctrine of grace were to be aired in Rome, Carthage and the East— indeed throughout the Roman world—in the early decades of the fifth century. In all his travels he was accompanied by his faithful friend, Celestius, a monk from Ireland, who acted as his mouthpiece and the interpreter of his teachings. This pair of companions, who seem to have been men of considerable charm, won a sympathetic hearing everywhere, particularly in the East, and it is not perhaps surprising that Pelagianism ultimately foundered on the rocks of humanism. Pelagius, who denied the doctrine of original sin as a legacy of our First Parents, proclaimed that man could, by his own efforts, perfect himself by faith and good works alone. Divine grace was present in every man, and he had only to use it aright to secure his salvation. It followed that those who had lived before Christ, no less than those whom He had redeemed by His sacrifice, had been similarly capable of perfecting them-selves by the use of their free will. Thus Pelagius, in effect, queried the whole purpose and efficacy of the Redemption. Against this threat to orthodoxy, Augustine opposed his own doctrine of grace.

According to Augustine, every man was born in original sin as a result of the Fall, and could only achieve the state of grace by virtue of the Redemption and the sacrament of Baptism. Thus he defended the practice of infant baptism, since the infant, though not wilfully sinful before his baptism, was so by nature through his very humanity. Those called to membership of Christ's Church were the recipients of God's grace which could itself be renewed and strengthened through the sacraments, and to such men salvation was predestined for all eternity. Grace was, in fact, irresistible, and though Augustine did not deny man's free will, he would not really allow him freedom of choice. This doctrine has never been accepted in its entirety by the Church, and indeed its rigorous logic suggests an *ad hoc* doctrinal position taken up in opposi-tion to extreme Pelagianism. Nowadays, although it is accepted that a man's membership of the Church is due to an initial, or prevenient grace, his success or failure to win salvation depends on the use of his free will in accepting or rejecting the graces made available to him during his lifetime. Pelagianism was not finally condemned until the Council of Ephesus in 431, and in its broader outlines it still exerts a not inconsiderable influence today.

In many ways, the heresy of Nestorius can be seen as a result of the decisions taken against Arianism at Constantinople in 381. Christ's position, as equal to that of the Father, had been defined. The new controversy hinged on the relationship in the One Person of Christ between His human and divine natures. Following the heresy of Theodore of Mopsuestia, that Christ was a man become God, Nestorius, a priest of the neighbouring city of Antioch, asserted that because God had become incarnate at a given moment in time, His Mother was therefore entitled, not to the title of Mother of God (*Theotokos*), but only of Mother of Christ (*Christotokos*). This was tantamount to an identification of the two natures in Christ with two separate persons, of whom the Virgin was Mother of only one. This heresy was opposed not only in Constantinople, where Nestorius had succeeded to the patriarchate, but especially in Alexandria, where the bishop Cyril stressed the Oneness of Christ's Person, in which the human and divine natures were united in identity of common experience. Cyril taught that the only Person which persisted through the Incarnation was that of God the Son; therefore, Christ's Mother was, in truth, Mother of God. The dispute was referred to Pope Celestine by both parties, in 429 by Cyril, and by Nestorius in the following year. Moreover, the situation was aggravated by the age-long rivalry between Alexandria and Antioch, whose bishop John regarded Cyril himself as a heretic. In 430 the Pope acted, by summoning a Council for which he nominated Cyril as Roman delegate; at the same time, he wrote to Nestorius bidding him renounce his heresy. Thereupon, Cyril informed Nestorius of the Pope's decisions, and forwarded a document, comprising twelve articles, which he (Nestorius) was required to sign in token of renunciation of his heresy. The next move was, however, taken by the Emperor, Theodosius II, who himself ordained another Council, to be held at Ephesus in 431 under the presidency of John, bishop of Antioch. In the meantime he enjoined silence on Cyril and Nestorius. To this Council the Pope agreed to send delegates; but on Whit Sunday, the day on which the Council was due to open, neither they nor the party from Antioch, including John, had arrived. Notwithstanding, Cyril proceeded to declare the proceedings open, himself took the chair and secured the con﹍demnation of Nestorius *in absentia*.

A fortnight later, John of Antioch arrived at Ephesus with thirty﹍seven bishops. John, not unnaturally furious at Cyril's high﹍handed actions, immediately called a rival Council, at which Cyril and those bishops who had supported him were anathematized; and in the middle of this operatic situation the Papal delegates arrived. A second session of the original Council was then called, and the findings of the first session reaffirmed. John and his followers were then excommunicated in their turn, and the delegates went their several ways. The Emperor, by this time in a state of understandable confusion, ordered the arrest of both Cyril and Nestorius. Like Pope Celestine himself, he refused to accept the excommunication of John of Antioch, and the whole unfortunate business only came to an end two years after Ephesus, when Cyril at last agreed to phrase his own doctrine in terms acceptable to Antioch. In this way a schism between two major patriarchates was avoided.

The victory of Cyril's Christology at the Council of Ephesus was actually a contributory cause of a new heresy. Eutyches, a monk of Constantinople, considering that Cyril had not gone far enough in condemnation of Nestorianism in his final compromise with Antioch, now declared that Christ, though consubstantial with the Father according to His divine nature, was not consubstantial with man according to His human nature. It followed that Christ therefore had only one nature, the divine. Eutyches' Monophysite (single nature) heresy was immediately accepted by Dioscurus, patriarch of

Alexandria, and neither he nor his flock ever afterwards wavered in their support. To Alexandria, Eutyches' teaching was seen as anti-Nestorian and, therefore, as a full vindication of their own bishop Cyril's position in the earlier dispute. The Emperor too came out on the side of the Monophysites, but Flavian, Patriarch of Constantinople, unexpectedly opposed them. The great champion of orthodoxy, however, was that outstanding Pope, Leo the Great, a man of the highest intellectual gifts as well as of personal bravery. In 449 the Pope issued a statement on the duality of Christ's nature in a single Person, but this was rejected without even being given a hearing by the so-called Robber Council of Ephesus, at which Dioscurus of Alexandria presided over a meeting packed with his own supporters. The Pope himself was declared to be excommunicated (!), while Flavian, orthodox patriarch of Constantinople, was deposed, imprisoned, and so maltreated that he died. Heresy seemed to have triumphed, and the prestige of Rome was at a very low ebb. For several months the Emperor systematically ignored Leo's letters of protest, and when finally he did deign to reply, it was only to confirm his support for the decisions of the Robber Council. In 450, however, Theodosius was killed in a riding accident, and was succeeded by his sister Pulcheria, an orthodox Catholic, who shared the throne with her husband Marcianus, also a Catholic. The way was now open to a re-examination of the Mono-physite heresy, and a Council was convened in Chalcedon in the autumn of 451. This time the decisions of the Robber Council of Ephesus were reversed; Dioscorus of Alexandria was excommunicated for his support of Eutyches and sent into exile, while Leo's 'Tome', a statement of orthodox dogma, was accepted as binding on the Church. However, as if to exact a *quid pro quo* from the Papacy, the Council also raised the status of the Patriarch of Constantinople (as being the first city of Christendom) to something approaching that of the Pope in the West. This decision was contested by the papal represen/ tatives; but the Council remained adamant, and when Leo wrote personally to signify his disapproval, he was met with evasion by the Patriarch.

Meanwhile events were moving fast, and in Syria, Palestine and Alexandria there was open revolt against Chalcedon. An uneasy truce between the Empire and the Papacy barely sur/ vived the collapse of the Roman Empire in the West, and when, in 482, the Emperor Zeno reached an accommodation with the Monophysites in the interests of political unity, the breach was complete, and remained so until the death in 518 of his successor Anastasius, himself a convinced Monophysite.

While the Church was busy with its own affairs, the world had not stood still. The triumphant march of the Gothic invader, halted on the very outskirts of Constantinople at the end of the fourth century, ended in the sack of Rome in 410. Forty years later, Attila the Hun was turned aside from the same objective by the personal intervention of the reigning Pope, Leo the Great, who yet lived to see Rome again occupied in 455, this time by the Vandals. Within the city itself, the barbarians ruled supreme, setting up and deposing puppet Emperors at will, yet somehow still awed into acceptance of the shadow of the old Roman order. In 476, the final blow fell, with the abdication of the pathetically named Romulus Augustulus, the last of the Emperors of Rome. A chapter of history, occupying more than a millennium, was at an end. Another, even longer, and whose end cannot be foreseen, is still in being.

Even as the clouds gathered over the Empire of the West, Christianity, its new vital force, was penetrating the dark corners of Europe to which Imperial Rome had never been much more than a name of power. In 397, Ninian founded his missionary church, the *Candida Casa* (modern Whithorn) in his native Galloway, in southern Scotland. Like many another young ecclesiastic, eager to visit the fountainhead of Western Christendom, Ninian studied for some years at Rome. There he was consecrated bishop, and before returning home to establish his mission in Southern Scotland, spent some time at the feet of St Martin of Tours, now an old man, in his monas-tery at Marmoutier on the Loire. In Ireland, the ministry of Patrick the Briton covered part of the fifth century, but owing to some confusion in the early sources it is impossible to be precise about his actual dates. All tradition supports Patrick as the man mainly responsible for the conversion of Ireland but, as the de Paors have pointed out, it is at any rate doubtful whether the country was entirely pagan before his arrival. Such evidence as exists is slender, but on the whole convincing. Apart from a persistent tradition of pre-Patrician Christianity in southern Ireland, Prosper of Aquitaine speaks of Palladius (Patrick?) having been sent in 431 by Pope Celestine to 'those of the Irish who believed in Christ', while Patrick in his own *Confessio* mentions remote parts of Ireland 'where never had anyone come to baptize or ordain clergy or confirm the people'. Unfortunately, archaeology is silent on early Irish Christianity until the seventh century.

While in the north-west the expansion of Christianity seems often to be shrouded in an Atlantic mist which sometimes lifts for a moment to reveal the vital figure of a Ninian or a Patrick, its progress in the East beyond the imperial frontier took place, as it were, in the full sunlight, against a background of well documented historical events which were to shape the Church's destinies for centuries to come.

The most influential area in the eastward march of Christianity was most certainly that comprised in the so-called Edessa–Amida–Nisibis triangle which, though nominally subject to the jurisdiction of Antioch, acted as a focal point for the Churches in East Syria and Persia and for the development of the Syriac liturgy. How successful its mission to Iran must have been is reflected in the vast number of Persians martyred during the persecutions of Shapur II, but with the king's death in 379 separatist tendencies began to show themselves, and in 424 the Persian Church declared itself independent of Antioch, with the seat of its *katholikos* at Seleucea Ctesiphon. In 431, both Persian and East Syrian Christians reacted against the condemnation of Nestorius at Ephesus, and just over fifty years later the Persian Church confirmed its attitude. Thereafter, no Christian body in history has ever surpassed the missionary activity of the Nestorians of East Syria and Persia. The Christians of the Malabar Coast of India, who claimed to be the disciples of the Apostle Thomas when they were re-discovered by the Portuguese at the end of the sixteenth century, were probably evangelized by them, and it was Nestorian missionaries for certain who penetrated the Chinese Empire in the seventh century. In the fourteenth century, as the Tartar hordes swept through Asia under Tamerlane, all this great achievement was to be swept away, and now the so-called Assyrian Church, with a total membership of little more than fifty thousand, is all that remains.

Christianity was accepted as the state religion of the Armenians at the end of the third century, and has ever since been most tenaciously defended. Indeed of no people, with the exception of the Jews, may it fairly be said that nationality and faith are so closely identified. At the beginning, the Church was dependent on the see of Caesarea in Cappadocia, whose bishop had ordained Armenia's first great churchman, Gregory the Illuminator, to the charge of the new converts, but this allegiance was cast aside in 374. Within a few years Armenia was occupied by the Persians, but bitter persecution acted as a spur to a sort of Christian nationalism. First, an Armenian alphabet was invented, and after the Scriptures had been translated into the vernacular, a new liturgy came into being. Political repression prevented the attendance of an

Armenian delegation to the Council which condemned Nestorianism at Ephesus; the Council of Chalcedon likewise passed the Armenians by. It was perhaps a natural reaction to the indifference of the Empire to their plight that led them to reject Chalcedon, and that the leanings of their enemies towards Nestorianism should have decided them in favour of Eutyches' heresy. At all events, except for an interlude when communion with Rome was established by the rulers of the medieval Cilician Kingdom of Little Armenia, the Church has remained, nominally, monophysite. Always inward-turning, as befits a nationally conscious people, the Armenian Church, whether Uniate or schismatic, has never lost its unique character.

Another branch of Christendom, established outside Roman imperial territories and which has since successfully survived in almost complete isolation, is the Ethiopian. Originally evangelized from Alexandria in the fourth century, it very naturally followed its parent church into heresy at the height of the monophysite controversy in the fifth century. A new mission sent to Ethiopia under Justinian founded a new Christian centre at Aksum, which still keeps its status as the holy city *par excellence*. Today, the Ethiopian Church, despite the accretion of many strange usages and the loss of contact with many other Christian bodies, still remains in association with the Coptic Church of Egypt, and to that extent may be described as monophysite.

Even nowadays, Christianity is all too often considered, quite wrongly, as a Western heritage, or still worse, as an exclusive Western privilege. Such a view might even seem to be well grounded, if outward appearances were the only guide; for the spectacle of the Churches of Egypt and the Near East, struggling in isolation or in an atmosphere of indifference from their more fortunate co-religionists is all too often unknown or ignored. Indeed resentment is sometimes heard at the presence of Christians of unfamiliar Churches in the occupation of different parts of the Church of the Holy Sepulchre at Jerusalem. Of course it does, in one sense, epitomize the sad situation of a divided Christendom, but there is some consolation in the fact that all Christians, Eastern and Western alike, should still think it so important to have even a small stake in the place universally identified with the supreme triumph of the Christian religion.

CHAPTER V

The Christian Basilica

JUST AS THE razing of a church in 303 had been the signal
for the beginning of the worst persecution of Christians
ever known, so some twenty years later Constantine's foundation of the church of St John Lateran in Rome symbolized the
dawn of a new era. The church was a basilica, and almost
immediately in Rome and in the eastern provinces it was
followed by other imperial foundations of the same basic plan.
Indeed, in all the main centres of Christendom, the basilica
seems rapidly to have supplanted the house-church and whatever other specialized buildings there may have been.

What, we may well ask, was the reason for this sudden
emergence of a fully developed and suitable church plan? A
number of answers to the question have been proposed in the
past, of which two at present command most support. The
first, and more popular, view is that the basilical church
represents the final stage in an architectural evolution to which
several earlier types of building, and notably the Roman civic
basilica, made their contribution; the second, cogently argued
by J. B. Ward-Perkins in a recent article (*Papers of the British
School at Rome*, Vol. XXII, 1954, pp. 69–90) is that its form was
inspired by the halls of audience in the imperial palaces which,
particularly under Constantine, acted as a setting for the
elaborate court ceremonial that was later partially absorbed into
the Christian liturgy. As a corollary to the second theory, it is
sometimes claimed that Constantine himself, either by precept,
example, or both, imposed the basilical plan as something like
a fixed standard on the newly liberated Church. The truth
probably lies somewhere between these two extremes. But
before discussing these and other, less likely answers to the
problem of its origins, a reasonably broad definition must be

found of the Christian basilica, a definition moreover that covers the salient features of churches falling within the category, but avoids details of a purely temporary or local significance.

Reduced to its simplest terms, the basilical church was an oblong hall of assembly with the emphasis along the main axis, and so on the semicircular apsidal recess that projected from one of the short sides. Internally, it was divided by two (occasionally four) rows of columns or other supports into a central nave flanked by side aisles. The outer walls, including that of the apse, were blank, so that apart from the little light that could filter through the doors, illumination depended entirely on windows in the clerestory that rose above the nave. This lack of direct lighting was in no way a disadvantage; rather it must have enhanced the flickering glow of candles and lamps against which the liturgical drama was enacted. The nave was covered with a double-pitched (gabled) roof, with a single-pitched roof over the aisles. There was a semi-dome over the apse.

The argument that such buildings were the natural outcome of centuries of evolution is largely based on the fact that many of the features just described were also present in certain civic basilicas which, with half a millennium of development behind them, were in general use all over the Roman world as town-halls, markets and law-courts. But while it is likely, indeed probable, that the long-aisled type of civil basilica exerted no small influence on the architects of the first basilical churches, it must be remembered that it was only one of several, since in the fourth century A.D. the word 'basilica' was often loosely applied to any public hall of assembly, apparently regardless of architectural considerations. To suggest the derivation of the basilical church from the civic basilica in its most general terms of application would, therefore, be quite erroneous; the choice of the long-aisled basilica as a model (if

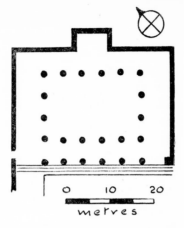

Fig. 16 Civic basilica at Cosa in southern Etruria. An early example of the centralized 'Italian' type. Second century B.C.

such a choice was consciously made) must *a priori* have been due to its special suitability for housing a Christian congregation.

In Republican times the word 'basilica' was most probably understood in the specialized sense used by the Augustan architect Vitruvius in describing a building which he planned for the Adriatic town of Fanum (Fano). It was rectangular, with a central ambulatory and clerestory lighting; the lateral axis was emphasized, with the entrance in the middle of one of the long sides. Opposite this door was a recess, the *tribunal* of the presiding magistrate or other official. Recent excavations at the coastal site of Cosa in Etruria have shown that a basilica of the Vitruvian type existed there in the second century B.C., and two similar examples of the later Republican period are known from Ardea and Alba Fucens. During the Imperial period, this broad, centralized basilica, often with one of its long sides flanking the forum, had a wide distribution, particularly in Italy and the western provinces. At Rome the Ulpian basilica built under Trajan in 114 is an outstanding example of this type, while outside Italy almost any settlement large enough to boast a civic centre had its own basilica, even

Fig. 16

down to the little British tribal capital of Calleva Atrebatum (the modern Silchester in Hampshire).

The origin of this type of basilica has been much disputed. It has been suggested that the name itself was derived from the *Stoa Basileios*, the royal audience hall of the Ptolemies in Hellenistic Egypt. If so, the use of the word in Italy must have been based on some supposed similarity of function in the Greek *stoa*, or portico, and the Italian hall of assembly, since architecturally they have nothing in common, except in the use of columns. It is, of course, conceivable that the term *stoa* was applied in Alexandria to the traditional non-Greek hypostyle hall of earlier Egypt, but this would suggest the existence of such a building in the palace of the Ptolemies, and there is no evidence for it. However, a centralized plan is characteristic of Oriental architecture, and it is possible that the centralized type of basilica reached Italy through such an intermediary as the famous Hellenistic hypostyle hall at Delos. Leroux quite simply calls the centralized basilica 'Oriental', but since the type is far commoner in the West than in the East, it is perhaps more convenient (while leaving open the question of ultimate provenance) to describe it as 'Italian'.

However, despite its interior colonnades, its clerestory and *tribunal*, the Italian civic basilica could never have influenced the plan of the first basilical churches, since in the latter the longitudinal disposition of the building was of the essence, as it was earlier in the Greek temple *cella* and, even before, in the pre-Hellenic *megaron*. It is in fact likely that the influence of an Eastern Mediterranean tradition upon the fundamentally simple plan of a closed building with internal colonnades led to the evolution of the long-aisled civic basilica, which in its turn may have suggested to Constantine's architects the idea of a basilical hall incorporated in the Emperor's first and most important foundations.

Interesting as something of an architectural landmark is the

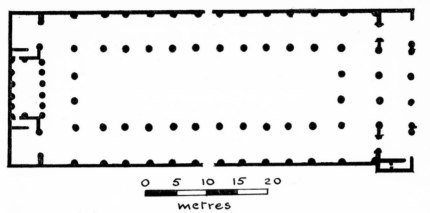

Fig. 17   Civic basilica at Pompeii, with the main emphasis on the longitudinal axis. First century B.C.

civic basilica built at the beginning of the first century B.C. at Pompeii; for although the centralized arrangement was in fact maintained, with a door in the middle of both the long sides, the real emphasis was on the longitudinal axis. The main access to the forum was through one of the short sides, and so the vista towards a raised *tribunal* at the far end of a double row of columns was stressed rather than the lateral disposition of the central ambulatory. Here in near-Greek Campania, the architect seems to have aimed at a compromise between the Italian type of basilica and some Hellenistic prototype like the third-century version of the temple of the Cabiri in Samothrace, which had a double row of columns culminating in an inscribed apse. The basilica at Pompeii was certainly without a clerestory and may well have had a flat roof. It is most unlikely that the central area enclosed by the colonnades was open to the sky, as some have supposed. If it had been, the building would have had no more relevance to the origin of the Christian basilica than Dyggve's so-called *basilica discoperta* at Marusinac. Granted, however, that it was roofed, then it is obviously closer—despite its lack of a clerestory and a projecting *tribunal*—

Fig. 1

129

in the line of development to the basilical church than any Italian basilica pure and simple, however well equipped otherwise with relevant architectural features. This is, of course, much truer of long-aisled basilicas designed as such, from the Hadrianic example at Cremna in Pisidia to the basilicas of Maxentius and Constantine at Rome and Trèves respectively. At Lepcis Magna in Tripolitania, the Severan basilica was ultimately turned into a church in Justinian's time, after one of the four rooms at the corners of the main hall had been used as a synagogue during the preceding century. All the same, this is an isolated instance of such a transformation, and very few civic basilicas are known to have been adapted for use as churches. On such grounds the argument is sometimes rather unreasonably advanced that there can have been little archi-tectural connexion between the two. This is surely to overlook the continued necessity for town-halls, covered markets and law-courts, even after the adoption of Christianity as the state religion.

The only large buildings to become outmoded as the Church grew in membership and authority were the pagan temples; but the Empire was not converted overnight, and many temples survived alongside the new churches. Even as late as 529, when Justinian closed the University of Athens, there were still 'several pagan professors . . . leading an obscure existence' in the city. Gradually, however, and specially in Asia Minor, where Christianity had very early won a strong following, a number of temples were taken over by the Church. Despite the obvious unsuitability of their original plan—they were designed to house a cult statue and not a congregation engaged in a corporate act of worship—they had their advan-tages, specially for less wealthy communities, who found in them a cheap source of cut stone, ready to hand. Moreover, while providing a welcome continuity of religious associations for the local populace, the re-dedication of the building to

Plate 3
Fig. 37

Christ exorcized the pagan gods, now become demons, of the old pantheon.

Methods used to adapt a temple to suit its new purpose varied according to local conditions, but were always aimed at producing a plan approximating as nearly as possible to that of a basilical church. Much, too, depended on the size of the prospective congregation. At Aphrodisias in Caria, where a large church was needed, the *cella* of the temple of Aphrodite was demolished. New walls were built beyond the peripteral colonnade (which now became the inner order) and an apse was thrown out at the east end. At Elaeusa Sebaste in Cilicia, on the other hand, the population of the port was diminishing due to a gradual silting up of the harbour. Consequently only one corner of the pagan temple was used for the new church built there in the fifth century.

The commonest adaptation was that employed at Diocae-sarea (Uzuncaburç) in Isauria, where the whole colonnade of the temple of Olbian Zeus was filled with masonry to form the outer walls, and an apse added at the east end; the *cella* walls were removed, and replaced by a double row of supports, for which the only surviving evidence is a pair of responds jutting out from the east wall, on either side of the apse. These supports divided the interior into a nave and two aisles. This example was later followed in the West, for example in the seventh-century cathedral at Syracuse; here, however, the *cella* walls of the temple of Athena were pierced by arches, thus preserving the illusion of two rows of internal supports. All these examples go to show that the theory of a direct influence by the Greek temple on the Christian basilica is untenable. As Cecil Stewart has said: 'it was as though the Greek temple were turned inside out' (*Simpson's History of Architectural Development*, Vol. II, p. 9).

A much better case can be made out for the part played in the evolution of the basilical church by other pagan places of

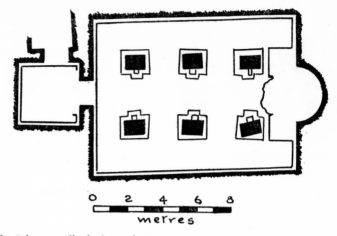

Fig. 18   Subterranean 'basilica' near the Porta Maggiore in Rome. First century A.D.

worship intended for the celebration of rites before a congregation. In this connexion, the subterranean 'basilica' near the
Porta Maggiore in Rome and a number of Mithraea from Italy
to northern Britain are the most relevant.

The subterranean 'basilica', which probably dates from the
first century A.D. was built of concrete, and has many remarkable similarities to some early basilical churches. Its two rows
of piers—three on each side along the main axis—were connected by arches, and divided the temple into a nave and two
aisles. There was a semicircular apsidal recess at the west end,
roofed by a semi-dome, while the nave and aisles were barrel-
vaulted. The 'basilica', which was decorated with elaborate,
but enigmatic wall-paintings on plaster, cannot be positively
identified as the meeting place of any known sect. Unique as
it is, it would be most unwise to claim for this building any
special role or influence on early church architecture, though in
it many features of the Christian basilica are anticipated. Had
it been used by Christians, there can be little doubt that it
would have been hailed as a prototype!

Temples of Mithra, wherever in the Roman world they have been discovered, generally conform to a set plan, of which the Mithraeum below the church of S. Clemente in Rome may be taken as representative. Basically, the temple was a long rectangular crypt with benches of masonry down the long sides. On these the congregation sat or reclined, with a narrow passage separating them. The place of sacrifice, at the far end of the building and facing the entrance, was railed off from the main body of the congregation, and its importance emphasized by a central altar adorned with reliefs of Mithra and the bull. Here again, although to a less marked degree than in the 'basilica' near the Porta Maggiore, are several points of contact, both in general and detail with the earliest developments in basilical church architecture.

Rather unusual, and specially interesting for comparative purposes, is the Walbrook Mithraeum in London. While it was still only partially cleared, with its attribution as yet uncertain, it was described by its excavator as 'part of a small temple of basilican plan . . . with an apse at the west end opening into a hall originally divided by arcades into a nave and two side aisles . . . '. As work proceeded, it became clear that the apse and aisles had originally been at a higher level than the nave, while at the east end a porch extending across the full width of the building (as so often in early Christian basilicas) was revealed. This Mithraeum was apparently in use from the turn of the second and third centuries A.D. until the time of Constantine at least. During this period, many of its architectural features were modified, including the removal of the arcades and the gradual raising of the floor level in the apse and side aisles. Finally, shortly before its abandonment, many fine sculptures, not only of Mithra but of many other pagan deities besides (e.g. Serapis, Minerva and Mercury), were carefully buried in the building to protect them from sacrilegious hands—very probably from the Christians.

Towards the close of the third century the cult of Mithra had become merged in that of the Sun—*Sol Invictus*. We know that a western orientation was normal in Constantinian basilicas, so that the rays of the rising sun fell upon the celebrant as he stood behind the altar facing the congregation. Many have seen in this a reminiscence of the Emperor's enthusiasm for sun-worship for many years after he officially championed Christianity. Considered against this background, it is not really surprising how closely the Walbrook Mithraeum corresponds in plan to some early Christian basilical churches. Indeed it seems easier to believe in the possibility of some direct Christian borrowing from pagan religious sources than to reject it.

Those who suggest that the choice of the basilica was due to a direct initiative of Constantine, and that he was influenced in that choice by the audience halls incorporated in the imperial palaces, very rightly stress in support of their theory the suddenness and speed with which this basically simple plan was adopted, and then spread during the fourth century throughout the Roman Empire. Indeed, so far as the choice of a specialized building is concerned, the imperial example in Rome, Constantinople, Jerusalem and Bethlehem may well have played a

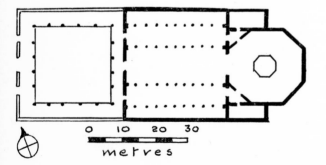

Fig. 19   The Church of the Nativity at Bethlehem, with octagonal memoria, *central basilical hall and western* atrium

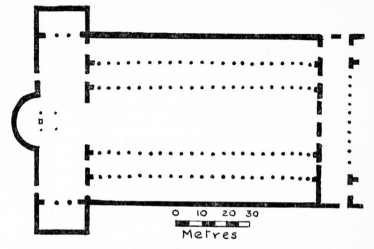

Fig. 20   The Constantinian basilica of St Peter in Rome was oriented to the West. The memoria *of the Saint may be seen on the chord of the apse, but the* atrium *to the east is not included in the plan*

decisive role; but in the present writer's view, it is far more likely that the basilical plan imposed itself on Constantine's architects than that it was consciously imposed by the Emperor on his Christian subjects. It is, in fact, quite reasonable to ask what type of building then in common use, other than the basilica, would have been so suitable or so readily adaptable to the needs of congregations attending the celebration of the Eucharist.

The churches founded by Constantine at Rome and Con-stantinople, at Bethlehem and Jerusalem were all basilicas, though they differ quite considerably between themselves in plan. At the Holy Places, sites were naturally chosen for their direct association with some important event in the life of Christ; and at Rome, the church of St Peter was built at the traditional place of the Apostle's martyrdom. That of St John Lateran, however, was built and dedicated without topo-graphical significance. Such factors played a considerable role in the plans of the churches concerned, since the architects of

Figs. 19, 20

churches in the first category had to allow for a special treatment of the *memoria*, the sacred spot which was the ultimate *raison d'etre* of their work. Thus at Bethlehem, in the Church of the Nativity, and in Old St Peter's in Rome, the basilical hall was not the whole church, but only the central element of three linked structures on the same longitudinal axis, all of which were units of the complete church. Both had a rectangular courtyard, or *atrium*, with colonnades, and this gave access to a basilical hall divided by rows of columns into a central nave and four side aisles. At Bethlehem the complex was completed by an octagonal structure covering the traditional birth-place of Our Lord, while in Old St Peter's the *memoria* of the Apostle stood on the chord of a projecting apse. In both churches each of the three parts of the building was a self-contained entity, and in the case of the *atrium* and basilical hall this is clear from the plans. The distinction between the hall and the *memoria* appears, in the case of Old St Peter's at least, far less marked. This tendency to see the *memoria* as a mere appendage to the basilical hall is probably due to a modern confusion of thought, brought about by later ecclesiastical practice where the reverence due to the Saints or to a holy place was brought into close relationship with the altar, which itself housed the sacred relics. In the early Church there was no such doubling of function; the *memoria* or *martyrium* often existed as a building in its own right, particularly in the East, while the altar might well be set up in the nave of the basilica. At Bethlehem, where the *memoria* was octagonal, the plan was unequivocal; in Old St Peter's it is harder to grasp; harder, despite the emphasis given by the addition of transepts, to dissociate the place of the *memoria* from that normally occupied later by an altar.

Until the sixteenth century, when the building of the present Renaissance church of St Peter resulted in the destruction of Constantine's basilica, Old St Peter's remained one of the best preserved of all early Christian foundations, and pilgrims were still able to read the words of the Emperor's dedication on the triumphal arch that spanned the west end of the nave.

'Since under Thy guidance the world has risen again triumphant to the stars, Constantine the Victor to Thee has raised this church.'

Not all Constantinian churches in Rome were built to the same elaborate specifications as Old St Peter's. St John Lateran, the titular church of the Bishop of Rome and the Emperor's first foundation in the capital, had no *memoria*, and its transepts seem to be a medieval addition to the simple three-aisled basilica. In any case, transepts were unnecessary, granted that in Old St Peter's they existed solely to provide a more effective setting for the *memoria* of the Apostle. On the other hand, the first church of St Paul Without the Walls followed the basic plan of Old St Peter's, and the three elements of *memoria*, basilical hall and *atrium* were all present. The *atrium*, with its central fountain (*cantharus*) for ritual ablutions, was a common feature of the early basilical churches of Rome, as it was elsewhere; but most of these Roman *atria* have now disappeared, and the sixth-century example at Parenzo in Istria is exceptional. Possibly due to the rising cost of building sites in Rome, the *atrium* seems to have lost popularity, and to have been replaced by a single portico (open to the outside and extending across the full width of the church) which had the function of a porch or vestibule. As for the *cantharus*, its function was retained by a washing-place in the vestibule, or in the *narthex* of Eastern churches. A good example of the latter is the recently excavated stone tank fed from a cistern in the western building of the fifth-century monastery complex at Alahan in Isauria.

Inside the normal Roman basilica, parallel rows of columns extended as far as the wall on either side of the apse or, in the

Plate 17

case of a building with transepts, as far as the transverse wall. In Old St Peter's and in S. Maria Maggiore, they carried the flat entablature of Classical tradition, and this supported the walls of the clerestory; in such churches, however, as St Paul's Without the Walls and S. Sabina, the columns were spanned by archivolts, and the walls rose above these. Such arcading, which seems to have first appeared in the colonnaded streets of the Eastern provinces and a little later in the palace of Dio-cletian at Split, made for the better lighting of the side aisles and also enhanced the elegance of the church interior as a whole. The timber beams of the clerestory roof were masked by a flat coffered ceiling which was elaborately decorated, some-times with precious metals, while the windows were either fitted with a grille or filled with pierced slabs of light stone or alabaster.

The transition from the horizontal emphasis of the main hall to the semi-dome of the sanctuary was effected by a transverse arch which spanned the whole width of the apsidal recess. This feature, known as the 'triumphal arch', normally stood to the full height of the church. Inside the apse, which was raised above the level of the nave and approached from it by steps, was the *confessio* (the successor of the *martyrium*), in which relics were preserved in an ossuary below the floor. The altar usually stood immediately above this, and at Dağ Pazarı in Isauria, a silver reliquary was found housed in a small rectangular recess below a circular marble slab set into the base of the altar itself. The apse, sometimes known as the *presby-terium*, was reserved for the clergy, and those not actually engaged in the service sat on a bench set against the wall and following its curve. In the centre, immediately behind the altar, was the bishop's throne. In front of the sanctuary and projecting into the nave was a marble balustrade of orthostats or lattice-work. This was the place of the choir, while the nave was often reserved for the minor orders. The main body of the congregation was confined to the side aisles, men to the south, women to the north. Catechumens and penitents remained out' side in the vestibule or, in the case of Eastern churches, in the *narthex*.

The walls of the clerestory, the spandrels of arches and the conch of the apse were frequently decorated with religious scenes in mosaic. Of these, the most important were usually reserved for the apse, as the focal point of the whole basilica. Geometric or iconographically 'neutral' subjects in mosaic were normal for floors which, alternatively, might be flagged, or paved with *opus Alexandrinum*, a technique whereby coloured stones and marbles were regularly shaped and fitted together to make up a geometric pattern.

The Roman basilica was, of course, a single variation on a common theme, and in Greece and the coastlands of Asia Minor, Anatolia, Syria, Mesopotamia, North Africa and Western Europe as far as Britain, although the plan was widely accepted as a standard for church architecture, local characteris' tics everywhere developed according to differing geographical factors and building materials. These variations in detail are often so numerous, even in a relatively small area, that it would be impossible to include them all in a short survey. Con' sequently, only the most important will be described here.

In Italy, many of the early basilicas remain in use as churches to this day, though inevitably with later accretions and restorations. In Greece, the surviving number is small, while in the old Christian world of the Near East, those few that remain in Christian hands (e.g. at Bethlehem and Jerusalem) have been almost entirely rebuilt. In Constantinople, churches which were taken over by the Moslem conquerors to serve as mosques remain relatively intact. Elsewhere in the Islamic lands, Christian archaeology is archaeology indeed, and the majority of the ruined monuments, often half or entirely buried, await the spade of the excavator.

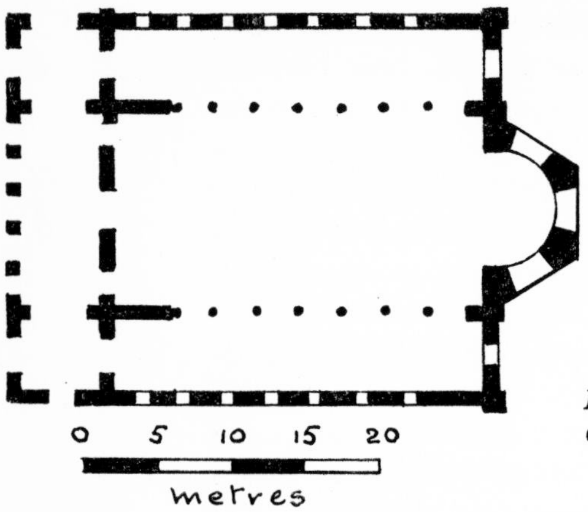

Fig. 21 Basilical church of St John Studion at Constantinople. Mid fifth century

The standard basilica of Greece and the Eastern Mediterranean differed little from the Roman type. However, arcading was the rule for internal colonnades, and galleries (*hyperoa*) for the accommodation of women above the side aisles were frequently provided. This feature, recalling the arrangement of some early synagogues, was present in the basilicas of St John Studion in Constantinople and of St Demetrius in Salonika, and is found all over the Mediterranean seaboard of Asia Minor. There, the monastery church of Alahan in Isauria provides a notable example. In Rome such galleries occur, exceptionally, in S. Agnese and S. Clemente, but these must be considered as examples of Oriental influence. The vestibule, though not unknown in the East (e.g. at Canytela in Cilicia), was usually replaced by the *narthex*, a porch extending the full width of the façade; unlike the vestibule, it was intended to give direct access to the church, while being closed to the outside. Courtyards are by no means uncommon, but in some areas, notably in Syria and eastern Cilicia, they were occasionally sited to the south of the basilica instead of in their usual position to the west, on the main axis of the building.

The treatment of the east end of normally oriented basilicas

Plate 26

in the East Mediterranean (or Hellenistic) group is the chief
source of variations in plan. In some (e.g. St John Studion) *Fig. 21*
the aisles ended, without elaboration, at the east wall of the
basilica, and at Ravenna, a city in close touch with the
Byzantine world, the plan of S. Apollinare Nuovo, completed
under Theodoric at the beginning of the sixth century, conforms to this principle. In coastal Asia Minor too the arrangement was usual, and standard in the case of basilicas which
resulted from the modification of pagan temples. More commonly, however, the east end was 'developed' to suit liturgical
and aesthetic requirements, and in a few isolated cases this
development took the form of transepts which gave to the
basilica a cruciform or near-cruciform plan. In Greece some
churches had transepts which were effectively closed to the
aisles by a transverse wall, thus following the tradition of such *Fig. 20*
Roman basilicas as Old St Peter's and St Paul Without the
Walls. In Asia Minor, however, where transepts were never
generally accepted by architects as a normal feature of the
basilical plan, they take a different, open form. Thus, in
'transept basilicas' at Corycus and Anazarbus in Cilicia, at
Sagalassus in Pisidia and in the church of St John at Ephesus,
there was no transverse wall to separate the aisles from the
transepts. The result was an open, cruciform plan, with the
transepts immediately accessible to the main body of the
church. A trefoil apse, found at Dodona in the Epirus and in a
number of churches in Lycia and Lycaonia, seems to be an
extension of this idea. It may appear strange that the 'transept
basilica' enjoyed so little favour in the East, especially in view
of the popularity of the cruciform plan for *martyria* at Binbir
Kilise (the Thousand and One Churches) in Lycaonia and
for rock-cut tombs in Syria. The truth is that the plan was more
suitable for the centralized type of building, with a dome at the
point of junction between the arms of the cross, as it is found
in the Mausoleum of Galla Placidia at Ravenna, or as it *Figs. 22, 23*

existed in Justinian's foundation, the Church of the Holy Apostles at Constantinople. Later, particularly in the familiar 'cross in square' form, the sacred symbol played a prominent role in the church plans of Greece, Macedonia and Asia Minor. The function of the transepts in the cruciform basilicas of the East is problematic. They certainly provided elbow-room for the clergy, and it may be that they were used as repositories for the gifts of the faithful, before the deacons offered them up at the rite of *prothesis*; but it cannot be proved that this was their primary purpose. Symbolic and aesthetic considerations were probably uppermost in the minds of the architects.

In Asia, the commonest method of developing the east end of the so-called Hellenistic basilica was to extend the north and south walls as far as, or beyond the point of, the apse, and then *Fig. 30* to complete the rectangle by joining these (e.g. the monastery church at Alahan). This arrangement left spaces on either side of the sanctuary, and these were variously treated. In some cases, the architects simply walled off the extra space at the end of the aisles, and so deliberately rejected the idea of using it for rooms flanking the apse. In others, where there was a clear space between the east wall and the outer curve of the apse, doors from the aisles gave access to a continuous room. Yet another plan, popular in Syria and Cilicia, provided for a single room to the north, and an open chapel to the south which may have done duty as a *martyrium*. By and large, however, the most usual arrangement was the so-called tripartite sanctuary, whereby the apse was flanked by a pair of symmetrical rooms with square or apsidal ends; these were entered from the aisles, and communicated by a side door with the sanctuary. Apart from their obvious convenience for storing church furniture and as a vestry for the clergy, it is likely that these rooms were also used from the first as *pastophoria*, or places for depositing the congregation's gifts of bread and wine for the Eucharist. Later, as the *diakonikon* and *prothesis,* their use became standardized for the preparation of the Offertory. Originating in northern Syria, the tripartite sanctuary was soon adopted in Cilicia (e.g. at Bodrum), though it is not found at Anazarbus, the second metropolis of the plain. The mid-fifth-century Council church at Ephesus is also equipped with *pastophoria,* and by the sixth century the tripartite sanctuary had spread westwards to Macedonia and Greece; there the externally rectangular plan did not maintain, since an apse projecting from the east wall was the rule.

Fig. 22 *Cruciform church (No. 8) at Binbir Kilise (Madenşehir) in Lycaonia*

Wherever in the East there was timber enough for roofing, and no native architectural tradition strong enough to challenge it, the Hellenistic basilica reigned supreme. It is present in Egypt, where it might reasonably have been expected to be crowded out by church buildings conforming to the ancient style of religious architecture. In North Africa, the plan was almost universally adopted. Local peculiarities there certainly were, in the form of a multiplicity of aisles, running to seven in the memorial church of St Cyprian at Carthage, and in the large basilica at Tipasa in Mauretania, where the number was later increased to nine. Moreover, several basilicas of otherwise normal plan in Africa Proconsularis were provided with an apse at either end of the building. In North Africa as a whole, details of construction show affinities not, as one might expect, with Rome, but with maritime Syria and eastern Cilicia, and such features as the inscribed apse flanked by *pastophoria* and galleries over the side aisles are very frequent.

Fig. 23 *'Mausoleum' of Galla Placidia at Ravenna. Mid fifth century*

Some churches of Anatolia, Mesopotamia, and Syria beyond the coastal regions are often classified, not entirely correctly, with basilicas. It is true that in Anatolia at least, the influence of the basilical plan with its stress on the longitudinal axis of the building was considerable, and that features like the apsidal recess and the *narthex* porch were borrowed direct from Hellenism. On the other hand, lack of timber led to the use of

143

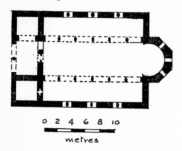

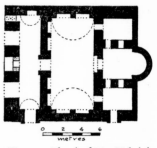

Fig. 24   Church No. 3 at Binbir Kilise (Madenşehir) in Lycaonia. The roofing of the nave and aisles was barrel vaulted

Fig. 25   Church of Mar Yakub (a so-called transverse basilica) at Salah in the Hauran district of Syria

Fig. 24

Fig. 25

stone for roofing, and the barrel-vaulted 'basilicas' of the Anatolian plateau are closely connected with the churches of Mesopotamia and parts of Syria which looked to the Orient for their architectural inspiration. At Binbir Kilise in Lycaonia, the stone barrel-vaults of the nave and aisles were supported by piers instead of columns, while the narthex was broken up into three compartments, of which only the central one had direct access into the nave. The vaulted roofs, of course, precluded the existence of a clerestory, and so the churches were illuminated instead by windows in the side aisles and in the apse. This form of lighting is found, as an import, in the church of S. Sabina in Rome.

Further still from any Hellenistic prototype is the so-called 'transverse basilica', a question-begging term if ever there was one. In the church of Mar Yakub in the Hauran district of Syria, although the *narthex*, apse and flanking *pastophoria* are present, the only concession to a longitudinal emphasis is provided by the doors with their continuous vista from porch to sanctuary. The 'nave' was a barrel-vaulted chamber stretch-ing the full width of the church, without internal divisions and at right angles to its main axis.

CHAPTER VI

Christian Centralized and Domed Architecture

THE CHIEF MERIT of the basilical church is its simplicity. With its clean lines and lack of any obvious
architectural artifice, no basilica can ever be vulgar. Yet, even
at its best, in such churches as S. Maria Maggiore or S. Apollinare in Classe, the plan has limitations. Once provided with a
dome, however, the basilica is transformed; so transformed
indeed, that it is a domed basilica, the church of St Sophia in
Constantinople, that marks the zenith in Christian architectural achievement of any place or age. This unique achievement
was made possible by the genius of its two architects, Isidorus
of Miletus and Anthemius of Tralles, working under the
patronage of Justinian; but before that time the stage had been
set, by experiments aimed at the fusion of two distinct
architectural ideas—that of the long-aisled Hellenistic basilica
described above, and the centralized building, often roofed
with a dome.

Plate 17

Plate 81

While the emphasis of the basilical church lies along its
main horizontal axis, and so on the sanctuary, in the centralized
building it is precisely the reverse, and the structure is rhythmically, and sometimes symmetrically ordered round the central
vertical axis. Thus the centralized building *par excellence* is of
circular plan, with its roof logically, though not of necessity, a
dome. That such buildings are known in the East as well as in
the West, and in particular that they existed in the Hellenistic
cities of the Eastern Mediterranean, has led some scholars to
join in the familiar game of 'Hunt the Oriental Prototype',
and to deny to Rome an original contribution in the field
of domical architecture. In fact, while the construction of

buildings incorporating a dome over a square bay, whether by the use of squinches or triangular pendentives, may very reasonably be accepted as an Oriental innovation, the Roman invention and use of concrete as a building material opened up immense possibilities for the treatment of large interior spaces unencumbered by standing supports, and not least for domical roofing of a fairly simple type. The combination of the circular plan with a dome resting on the outer wall is represented by that most magnificent of all Hadrianic buildings, the Pantheon, while the circular plan (possibly in this instance derived from Etruscan models) was also extensively used for funerary architecture, from relatively simple memorials to the more pretentious tomb of Caecilia Metella on the Appian Way and the vast mausolea of Augustus and Hadrian. The barbaric triumphal monument at Adamaklissi in the Dobruja is in the same tradition. At the same time, the architects of the great thermal establishments, like the Baths of Caracalla or of Diocletian (now the church of S. Maria degli Angeli), experimented with the construction of the dome over an octagon by means of 'false pendentives', a step towards the solution of the problem of the dome set over a square bay.

The triumph of Christianity did not mean the abandonment of the circular plan as suitable for some specialized religious buildings. Its commemorative purpose was maintained in its choice for the *martyria* which housed the relics of the saints and martyrs, or which covered sites specially associated with Christ, like the Constantinian foundation at Jerusalem over the traditional place of Our Lord's Resurrection—the Anastasis. The *memoria* of the Nativity at Bethlehem was, however, octagonal. Harking back to the domed rooms incorporated in the imperial bath buildings, were the circular and octagonal baptisteries of the West, such as S. Giovanni in Fonte in Rome, and others in Nocera, Ravenna, Albenga and Fréjus.

One of the most famous of all early Christian buildings in

*Fig. 26   Church of S. Costanza in Rome.
Possibly at first a mausoleum, it was
later a baptistery and finally a church.
Early fourth century*

0   5   10   15   20

metres

Rome, the circular building sometimes thought to have been
erected to house the sarcophagus of the Emperor Constantine's
daughter Constantina, who actually survived her father, is
now the church of S. Costanza. The plan is most interesting,
as it provides the first instance of a dome set upon a masonry
drum. This drum, which was pierced with twelve windows,
itself rested on a circular arcade of twelve pairs of columns,
each pair surmounted by a full entablature. The outward thrust
of the dome was taken up by a vaulted ambulatory which
almost encircles the building and of which the fourth-century
mosaic decoration still survives. The dome is not visible from
the outside, as the walls of the drum were continued high enough
for it to be roofed over with wood. A long porch with semicircular ends gave access to the single door. S. Costanza had
an immediate predecessor at Jerusalem in the Anastasis, or
memoria of the Resurrection, which was built to much the same
specifications, though it had the added feature of a triforium
above the ring of inner columns. Unlike S. Costanza, however,
it almost certainly had a wooden dome, as did the almost contemporary octagonal church at Antioch. Such a renowned
building as the Anastasis may well have influenced the architect

147

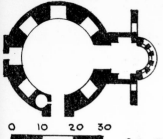

Fig. 27 Church of St George at Salonika, originally perhaps the Tomb of Galerius. The apse is a later addition to the original rotunda. Mid fifth century

of S. Costanza; that the reverse should be the case is clearly most unlikely.

Far simpler is the church of St George at Salonika, which was dedicated in the fifth century, after an apsidal sanctuary had been added to a circular Roman building, very possibly a *memoria* of the late pagan period. The original rotunda had a very thick outer wall into which, at ground level, were set eight large arched recesses of square ground plan. Above these niches, two of which acted as doors, were the windows. The dome itself rested directly on the outer wall which, like that of S. Costanza, was carried up and roofed with timber. The addition of an apsidal sanctuary became necessary when the building was taken into congregational use, and its light construction contrasts with the more ponderous mass of the Roman rotunda.

It may be said of both S. Costanza and St George that they are churches by accident rather than design, since the original purpose of each—to act as a *memoria*—was later obscured by their conversion for another function. Where baptisteries are concerned, however, the situation is quite different. Since the intimate nature of the baptismal ceremony made large buildings unnecessary, they were not really suitable for conversion into churches, and such an example as that of the fifth-century baptistery at Nocera near Naples is, in fact, a rarity. In any case, in the East the circular or octagonal baptistery is quite exceptional.

Apart from the one at Dura, the earliest known baptistery is that of St John Lateran (S. Giovanni in Fonte) which was prob-ably built under Constantine, but later underwent considerable alteration. Now, while the basic plan of S. Costanza is a circle within a circle—an example followed by the Nocera baptistery—that of S. Giovanni in Fonte is an octagon within an octagon, of which the inner portion consisted of eight porphyry columns topped by an architrave, itself supporting eight smaller columns which carried the lantern and, ultimately, the dome. Far more sophisticated is the fifth-century Baptistery of the Orthodox at Ravenna. Internally it is a domed octagon; but whereas in S. Costanza the outward thrust of the cupola was absorbed by a vaulted ambulatory, at Ravenna—where there is no interior order—it was taken up by four deep niche-buttresses which alternated with blind arches. In order to preserve the harmony of the interior, a blind arch, supported by engaged columns and pierced by a window, was constructed at a higher level on each of the eight sides, and above these the dome was constructed. The transition from the octagon was effected by false pendentives, with the angles between the walls continuing for a short distance upwards, before fanning out over the arches to form the ring on which the dome was built.

    Though Constantine's octagonal church at Antioch shows that such a plan was early considered suitable in the East for congregational use, and despite the fact that the niche-buttressed square surmounted by a dome was—if it had not already been adopted—in process of evolution in Armenia, the vast majority of early Christian octagonal and circular buildings in the Hellenistic East were *martyria*. At Bethlehem and Jerusalem, for example, basilical halls were added for the celebration of the Eucharist, but the prime function of the *martyrium* was kept entirely separate. In the West, this was not so, as is proved by the incorporation into the basilicas of St Peter and St Paul of the *memoriae* of the two Apostles. However, in the East the honour due to the relics of the saints and martyrs was not associated with the Eucharist until the early fifth century, and then, as remarked above, provision was

Plate 75

Fig. 19

Fig. 20

sometimes made for this by the addition of a special chapel
flanking the main apse of a normal basilical church. Nevertheless, such an arrangement was really a *pis aller* and made no
notable contribution to church architecture, and it is fortunate
that in some areas the influence of the traditional *martyrium* was
strong enough to effect a real transformation. Through it arose
the centralized churches of Palestine, Syria and Mesopotamia,
and since in such buildings the dome was a normal require-
ment, all the traditional skills of Oriental architects in domical
construction were brought into play. Finally, with the mastery
of the problem of constructing a cupola over a square, the
domed basilica became a possibility, and with it the architectural miracle of St Sophia.

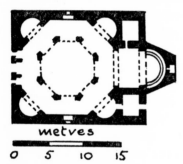

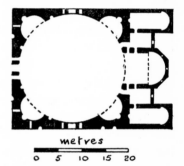

*Fig. 28   Church of St George at Ezra in
Syria. The plan is an octagon within a
square, with exedrae at the four angles.
Early sixth century*

*Fig. 29   Cathedral at Bosra in Syria.
The plan is a circle within a square, with
niche-buttressed exedrae at the corners.
Early sixth century*

Outstanding among the earlier centralized churches is that
built in 484 by the Emperor Zeno at Garizim in Samaria.
Essentially octagonal in plan, like a martyrium, its only
concession to a different liturgical purpose is an eastern apse.
Inside were eight piers, with two columns in each of the
intervals between them, except in front of the sanctuary, which

was thus left open. Above these supports the roof was, presumably, of wood. An interesting elaboration of the octagonal plan is provided by the church of St George at Ezra in Syria, which was built in 515–16. Here the octagon is inscribed in a square, with the four angles suitably filled by the insertion of *exedrae*, while an interior octagon of eight pillars linked by arches carried the dome. The plan was completed by the addition at the east end of two side chambers flanking a central, external apse. At Bosra, not far south, a similar idea lies behind the plan of the cathedral built in 512–13. This is basically a circle inscribed in a square, with *exedrae*—this time flanked by small niches—again filling up the angles.

The centralized churches of Armenia, first brought into prominence by the works of the Austrian scholar Strzygowski, occupy a somewhat enigmatic position in the history of early Christian architecture. On the one hand, in accordance with Strzygowski's tenets, Armenia is still sometimes considered the *fons et origo* of all domed Byzantine architecture, including S. Vitale in Ravenna and St Sophia in Constantinople; on the other, it remains a fact that no known church in Armenia antedates the period of Justinian. This lack of evidence might well be thought fatal to Strzygowski's arguments, but in fact they are not so easy to demolish. In the first place, not only was Armenia evangelized very early; it was actually the first country to adopt Christianity as the State religion—under Tiridates (261–316)—and churches must have existed from the outset. In the second, it may be argued that the highly distinctive Armenian church architecture that does survive, from however late a date, can only have reached so high a pitch of achievement as the result of development from prototypes which have so far eluded the archaeologist. This is, of course, special pleading, but it does not make it any the less difficult to refute.

Characteristic of one type of Armenian plan is the nichebuttressed square surmounted by a dome. In this case the niches project from the middle of all four sides of the square, as in the church of Mastara (*c.* 650), and sometimes niches are found at the corners also. A variation on the simpler type of niche-buttressed square is the cathedral of Bagaran (624–631) which encloses four central piers above which a dome was erected on squinches. A more or less logical development from the niche-buttressed square is the arrangement, represented by some seventh-century examples in Armenia, whereby the niches are contiguous, and so produce a quatrefoil or multifoil plan (consisting of six or eight lobes) which encloses a square, hexagonal or octagonal space as the case may be. From the octofoil variety of such churches Strzygowski derived the plan

Fig. 35

of S. Vitale at Ravenna, an opinion which, in view of the late date of the Armenian material, can only be regarded as speculative. In fact, there is reason to believe that in Italy itself the traditional architecture of Rome, in concert with elements derived from the Hellenistic world—itself not uninfluenced by the ancient capital—was capable independently of arriving at a plan far more complex than was achieved by the Armenian architects of a later period.

It will already have been noted that the domed *memoria* or baptistery of circular or octagonal plan was well within the competence of Roman architects of the Constantinian period, and also that such buildings followed a well-established tradition. If the plan of S. Costanza follows that of the Anastasis at Jerusalem, it is no cause for surprise, any more than that the basilical foundations of Constantine in both Asia and the West were fundamentally related. There was always a two-way current running between Rome and her Eastern provinces, and it is by no means easy accurately to determine whether any particular plan is an import, export, or even a re-export with elaborations derived from yet another source. In sixth-century

Fig. 35

Ravenna, the basilicas of S. Apollinare in Classe and S. Apollinare Nuovo strike no discordant note. S. Vitale, on the

other hand, seems almost to be the manifesto of a new architectural style, and its appearance in Italy with no apparent
intermediary between it and the earlier centralized Roman
buildings, would seem inexplicable except in terms of the
contemporary church of SS. Sergius and Bacchus in Constantinople or even as a result of the long-distance influence of
Syria and Armenia, where the relevant churches seem to have
appeared too late on the scene. Fortunately, however, such an
intermediary does exist in the form of the mid-fifth-century
church of S. Lorenzo in Milan, which has the unusual plan
of a quatrefoil in a niche-buttressed square with a tower at each
angle. The square central space enclosed by the quatrefoil was
almost certainly roofed by intersecting barrel-vaults, whose
thrust was absorbed, first by the angle towers, then by the
columnar *exedrae*, and finally by the vaulted ambulatory outside these. Such stout constructional methods strongly suggest
the survival of the Roman tradition as exemplified in S.
Costanza, but the use of columnar *exedrae* in Italy before this
time is rare. It is true that they existed in the Temple of Minerva
Medica in Rome, which actually led Strzygowski to suggest
that the building 'may be the work of Armenians'. However,
the columnar *exedrae* of the church in the stoa of Hadrian at
Athens and of the quatrefoil *martyrium* at Seleucea on the
Orontes are both of the fifth century, and the plan of the
martyrium, though structurally a much lighter building, much
resembles that of S. Lorenzo. It may well be that the columnar
exedra was a Hellenistic invention, though it is notable that the
earliest quatrefoil arrangement in an Eastern church, in the
cathedral at Bosra, belongs to the first quarter of the sixth   *Fig. 29*
century, about half a century later than S. Lorenzo.

The association of the cult of the martyrs with the celebration of
the Eucharist had led in Syria to the adoption of the centralized
church (often crowned by a timber dome) to which was added
an apsidal sanctuary in accordance with the requirements

of the liturgy. Coastal Asia Minor, however, remained faith-ful to the long-aisled basilica, and when, there also, the function of the *martyrium* became absorbed into a single church building, local architects refused to capitulate, but made a compromise on their own terms. This involved the retention of the basilical ground plan, with the single concession of a centralized superstructure which supplied the vertical stress required by the incorporation of the traditional *martyrium* into the architectural whole. Such a building is often described as a domed basilica, but this can be a misnomer, since in some cases—notably that of the monastery-church at Alahan in Isauria (formerly described as Koja Kalessi, and generally cited as a type specimen)—there was no dome at all. However, the question of whether or not the superstructure was crowned by a dome is not nearly as important as the idea underlying this type of church, the combination of a lateral and vertical emphasis which is the essence of such a building as St Sophia in Constantinople.

Plates 18, 19   The monastery at Alahan, sited on a rocky platform some three thousand feet above sea level on the pine-clad slopes of the Taurus, is one of the outstanding monuments of Early Christianity in Asia Minor, not only for its architectural quality but also for its fine sculpture. It is fairly securely dated to the mid fifth century by the epitaph of Tarasis, the guest-master, who died during February 462, and the church shows no signs of rebuilding. The ground plan is that of a normal

Fig. 30   Hellenistic basilica, with an inscribed apse flanked by *pasto-phoria*, and above the side aisles are the usual women's galleries. Just west of the sanctuary, however, four stout piers supported a rectangular tower which rises high above the pitched roof of the nave.

At each corner of this tower was a squinch arch, proving that the architects understood, even if they could not, or did not wish to apply, the principles governing domical construction

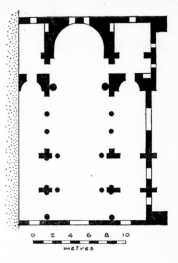

Fig. 30   Monastery-church at Alahan in Isauria. Long thought to be a 'domed basilica', it is now clear that it never had a stone cupola. Mid fifth century

over a rectangular bay. These squinches have given rise to considerable controversy; Strzygowski insisted that the church was domed, but in fact the thin walls of the tower could never have withstood the thrust of a masonry cupola. Furthermore, excavation proves that the tower was never roofed with any-thing more durable than wood. Forsyth is surely right in sug-gesting that 'the true solution is the simplest one, viz. a squat, pyramidal, wooden roof with flattened half pyramids at the corners'. The church at Meryemlik near Seleucea on the Calycadnus, often cited as a domed basilica, is equally suspect; so also is the recently excavated church at Dağ Pazarı (formerly, and wrongly, called Kestel), which in any case is an ambulatory church with a tower, and thus nearer in plan to the domed ambulatory church at Kasr ibn Wardan in north-east Syria than to the churches of Meryemlik or Alahan.

In order to meet the problems rising from the construction of a dome over a square bay, Early Christian architects normally employed one of two distinct methods, the squinch or the spherical triangular pendentive. The function of squinches is to transform a square plan into a many sided figure on which a dome may finally be constructed. This can be done either by laying flat slabs across the angles of the square (which thus

155

becomes an octagon), and repeating the process until the necessary foundation for a circular structure has been laid, or by building across the angles one or more arches superimposed above one another until the same effect is achieved. It is fairly certain that the squinch is of Eastern origin, and though it gradually lost popularity with the perfection of the pendentive, it continued to be used until the early Middle Ages.

The spherical triangular pendentive was a more sophisticated answer to the same problem. In itself, the pendentive is a masonry 'filling' between two adjacent arches, and in conse-quence is triangular in shape with an inward curve. In its most primitive form the curve of pendentive and dome is con-tinuous, and results in the so-called domical vault of which examples are common in Roman architecture. In such cases, the dome is not an independent entity. After some experiments on a relatively small scale, however, which were probably made first in Syria and Egypt, it became clear that if the pendentives were continued no higher than the crown of the arches, a continuous masonry ring resulted, on which an independent cupola could then be built.

CHAPTER VII

The Art of a Christian Empire

IF EARLY CHRISTIAN archaeology before Constantine is
largely confined to funerary monuments of a religious
minority at Rome and a few scattered sites elsewhere, after the
Edict of Toleration it is concerned rather with the achievements
and material possessions of the living; of men and women of
different races and traditions all over the Roman Empire and
the lands immediately outside it. On the physical plane, the
Christians of both periods lived just like their pagan contemporaries, and in their clothes, food, houses and furniture
they would not have differed from the rest of the community.
So, strictly speaking, any monument or object of the Christian
era from a site known to have numbered Christians among its
inhabitants is grist to the mill of the Christian archaeologist,
at any rate for comparative purposes. But the line must be
drawn somewhere, and in this book Christian archaeology is
taken to include material made for a specifically Christian
purpose (e.g. a church, an ambo or a thurible), or which was
earmarked for the use of a Christian owner by the use of
recognized symbols or iconography. Thus, for our purposes, a
lamp decorated with a chi-rho is Christian, while an exactly
similar lamp without the monogram is not. Such a categoriza-
tion, however arbitrary, has the merit of containing the
subject within reasonable bounds, and even so the amount
of material is embarrassingly large. Before Constantine, the
word 'art' is used, too freely perhaps, of almost any
Christian venture into stone-carving or painting. Later
on, one can be more selective, since in almost any category
of object or monument an example of outstanding merit is
easily found. Thus, this chapter, though properly concerned
with evidence regardless of aesthetic considerations, is also

intended to give an impression of the best work being done during our period.

The art of the Dura baptistery and of the Catacombs and early sculptured sarcophagi in Italy has shown how far the Christians had succeeded by the beginning of the fourth century in establishing a characteristic iconography. By Justinian's time, although many additions had been made to the repertory, chiefly in the form of scenes from the New Testament, especially the Passion, very little had dropped out, though some of the earlier symbolism gradually lost popularity, or became particularized. For example, the Good Shepherd is seen no more after the mosaic in the Mausoleum of Galla Placidia, while the seated philosopher with his roll or book becomes the Evangelist writing his Gospel, and the anonymous *orans* is personalized as a saint. After Constantine, Christian iconography not only became richer, but was employed with a greater subtlety, to emphasize points of doctrine rather than to tell a simple story. Meanwhile, many of the 'respectable' pagan symbols freely used in the earliest Christian art, continued in use, and the different schools of East and West persevered in their traditional methods. The first fusion of some of these was to take place under Justinian in the first Golden Age of Byzantine art.

Baptism into the Church entailed the obligation of attending celebrations of the Eucharist, and it was round the church building that the life of the Christian community quite naturally centred. And, just as a church was built to the greater glory of God, so its decoration and furniture had to be worthy of Him, regardless of expense. Various types of church have already been described previously, but what of their decoration? Leaving aside for the moment the architectural sculpture often found both inside and outside the building, the chief adorn- ment of the inner wall surfaces, flat and curved, were paintings executed in tempera, or mosaics. Floors were commonly paved with stone flags, *opus Alexandrinum* or, again, with mosaic.

Of painted decoration in early Christian churches not much survives, and Dura, already described, remains a notable exception. In churches of pre-Justinianic date, it has usually been obliterated by later work, while in those that are now ruined, the weather has attacked the plaster background and the stone casually thrown has hastened on its decay. In Egypt, the dry heat has helped to preserve some frescoes in small funerary chapels, but these mostly belong to the sixth century. Excavation, particularly in the Near East, might provide fresh evidence.

The paintings over the window lights in the Baptistery of the Orthodox in Ravenna consist of vine scrolls with winged deer and peacocks in grisaille, but these give little idea of the figured scenes from the Old and New Testaments that would have adorned many early churches. Their reflections may be seen, however, in illustrated manuscripts like the Vienna Genesis. Outside the churches and baptisteries, there are still the Cata-comb paintings, though after the Church had emerged from below ground, they were not representative of the best that Christian art had to offer. Of two examples of later Catacomb paintings, one will perhaps suffice to illustrate the survival of a factual Roman tradition, and the other of the intrusion of a fully 'expressionist' style which was a characteristic of Syrian art. The first is a Eucharistic scene, this time particularized as the Last Supper, with Our Lord a dominant figure in the centre of a sigma-table, with the Apostles seated round Him. There is no picturesque background, and the story is effectively, if simply, told. The frontal Madonna and Child from the Coemeterium Maius, however, is arresting in a stark and highly formalized manner. With its contrasts of light and shade, it explains too why the Syrians in their sculpture preferred the deep boring drill to the more even work of the chisel. A sixth-century Syrian ivory of the same subject, now in the British Museum, displays very similar characteristics.

Plate 75

Plate 11

Plate 16

It has been said that the first Christians were almost too fortunate in their artistic heritage; that is the view of those who believe that their art is no more than Classical art in decadence; that with all the spadework done in the past, there was no possibility of further advance. Where sculpture in the round is concerned, there is perhaps an arguable case; where wall and floor mosaics of churches and baptisteries are concerned, there is none. In this field, the Christian artist, though he built on the foundations of past achievement, gradually transformed the use of the medium to one specially suited to the expression of religious faith. Wall and floor mosaics cannot, however, be discussed together, because their treatment differed according to their different purposes, and also because in churches which have survived the floor mosaics have been worn out by genera∕tions of worshippers, while in those which have been destroyed and buried, the wall mosaics have disappeared even though the floors remain intact.

Owing to a complete lack of material evidence for Eastern Christendom during the fourth and the greater part of the fifth centuries, the earliest wall mosaics can only be studied in Italy, and chiefly in Rome and Ravenna at that. The picture is not, however, quite unbalanced, since the Italian mosaics were often influenced by Eastern Hellenistic art in general, and by Alexandrian in particular. The mosaics on the roof of the vaulted ambulatory of S. Costanza in Rome, which are contemporary with the building are a case in point. If this is, as is sometimes suggested, pre∕Christian, then the mosaics them∕selves will be pagan; but whether or not they are, it is interesting that at this time they are equally acceptable as Christian. The background to the mosaic, which is divided into panels by decorative borders, is white, in itself indicative of an early date. In later work, blue became popular, especially at Ravenna, while in mosaics of the full Byzantine period it is very often gold. The iconography of the panels, though not specifically

Christian, is none of it objectionable, and in any case it has parallels in undoubtedly Christian contexts of contemporary, or slightly later date. *Amores* at the vintage; interlinked roundels Plate 21 enclosing human heads, animals and birds; an elaborate arrangement of branches and flowers with birds and amphorae interspersed; all these form part of a Late Pagan–Early Christian repertory, derived from the Hellenistic East. Abstract decoration, with crosses and rosettes included in stellate and hexagonal figures, is, despite appearances, equally 'neutral' and, like the rest, suggests the influence of embroidered textiles. Of the dome mosaics nothing remains except the sixteenth-century painting of Francesco Olanda, which shows that the upper part was decorated with Biblical scenes chosen, apparently at random, and the lower with a river scene of *Amores* fishing, to which the fourth-century floor mosaic of the cathedral at Aquileia provides an obvious parallel. This Nilotic element, fore-shadowed in the second-century mosaics in the Palazzo Barberini in Palestrina, indicate that the ultimate provenance of the scene was probably Alexandria. In the two large niches of the church are two later works, intended to complement one another; the first is Moses receiving the tables of the Law on Mount Sinai, while the other is the *Traditio Legis*, the symbolic entrusting of the New Law by Our Lord to St Peter.

Less than a century probably divides the enigmatic mosaics of the ambulatory of S. Costanza from the apse mosaics of S. Pudenziana, also in Rome; in spirit they are separated by a world, for the latter is not only manifestly Christian, but is profoundly religious in atmosphere. The background has an almost magical quality. Above the city of Jerusalem—the free Jerusalem which 'is mother of us all'—dominated by the cross exalted above the hill of Golgotha, the four beasts of Ezekiel's vision look down on Christ enthroned. Seated on either side of Him are the Apostles; to His left is St Peter, attended by a female figure, representing the Church of the Circumcision, who offers him a crown; on His right is St Paul with a similar female figure, this time representing the Church of the Gentiles. Here is a scene in which heaven meets earth in incomparable majesty, and is not the less effective for its studied arrangement, with an over-all balance that misses the deadening quality of an absolute symmetry. The mosaics have, it is true, been much restored, but without apparently affecting their general impact on the viewer. Stylistically, there is much that recalls Pompeii; the architectural background and the allegorical figures of the two Churches are traditionally Hellenistic. The bearded Christ, here seen for the first time in the West, suggests the influence of the Orient.

The mosaics in the nave and on the triumphal arch of the basilica of S. Maria Maggiore were probably executed during the pontificate of Sixtus III (432–440), and represent a com-plete breakaway from the mystical side of Christianity as expressed in S. Pudenziana. In the nave, above the inter-columniations and in the spaces between the clerestory windows, are separate panels, each one portraying a scene from the Old Testament; on the triumphal arch, is a series of connected episodes in the life of the Virgin. The Old Testament scenes anticipate, in a sense, the famous 'Poor Man's Bible', whereby Christians became familiar with the scriptural stories by means of pictures, while in the events involving the life of the Virgin, probably based on the Apocryphal Gospel of St Matthew, the dogmatic element is to the fore. If correctly dated, these latter mosaics will have been executed just after the honour due to the Mother of God had been formally declared at the Council of Ephesus, where Nestorianism was condemned. Despite the great differences in style between the two sets of mosaics, both may be fairly described as 'Roman'; for though there is often a picturesque background to the stories of the Patriarchs, of Moses and of Joshua, the factual and narrative aspect is stressed, while the Virgin's life is represented in the 'continuous' style, associated with Roman art from the first century B.C., and specially familiar in the reliefs on the columns of Trajan and Marcus Aurelius.

The so-called Mausoleum of Galla Placidia at Ravenna is to be dated to about 450, during the short period that the city was the capital of the Western Empire. It houses three sarcophagi, once thought to be those of Constantius, Galla Placidia and her son, Valentinian III, but this view is no longer held. The little cruciform building may have been, as Laurent suggested, a *martyrium* of St Lawrence, since that saint is the subject of one of the major mosaics. Close ties with Constantinople, then 'senior' capital of the Empire, are responsible for what might be described as the proto-Byzantine style of its mosaics which, being all of one period and perfectly preserved, make the building a most valuable repository of Early Christian art. On the vaulted ceilings of the transepts are vine and acanthus scrolls against a background of dark, but brilliant blue, while in the lunettes at either end two deer confront each other across a stream. The east-west barrel vaults are decorated with petalled and pointed rosettes, like so many enlarged snow crystals against the deep blue of the background. In the eastern lunette, St Lawrence, a cross over his right shoulder hastens eagerly towards the grill, the instrument of his martyr-dom, while over the entrance, in deliberate contrast, is a scene of complete repose. In the centre, the young, beardless Shepherd sits on a rock with His flock around Him. In His left hand He holds a pilgrim's staff, while with His right He fondles one of His sheep. The pastoral background, with its small trees and flowers, has a trimness that suggests the work of a city-dweller, more at home with landscape gardening than the real country-side. The schools of Alexandria and Antioch are both sug-gested as the source of inspiration for this scene, and everything, from the still classical figure of Christ to the picturesque

Fig. 23

Plate 6

Plate 68

background, confirms the general view, with the balance of probability in favour of Antioch. The intersection of the two barrel vaults is crowned with a cupola, decorated with a single cross, luminous against the blue background studded with stars—*caelum stellis fulgentibus aptum*—at the highest point. Here, as in S. Pudenziana, the new devotion to the symbol of the Redemption is apparent. At the four corners are the beasts of Ezekiel's vision.

Plate 75

The almost contemporary mosaics of the Baptistery of the Orthodox, or of Neon (bishop of Ravenna 451–473), so called to differentiate it from the Baptistery reserved for his Arian co-religionists by Theodoric the Goth, have little in common with those of the Mausoleum of Galla Placidia. For where the art of the latter achieves its effect through concentration and a comparatively sparing use of colours, the mosaics of the Baptistery impress by their lavish polychrome and a diffusion which demands an ever closer attention. In the centre of the dome, a roundel containing a scene of Christ's baptism in the Jordan is encircled by the twelve Apostles against a blue ground. Below them, in eight separate panels that correspond to the facets of the octagonal ground plan of the building, are small architectural compositions, each one consisting of a columnar *exedra* flanked by a niche containing a richly cushioned chair. Every alternate *exedra* is filled by an elaborately canopied throne, while in each of the others is an altar, on which rests an Evangeliary, St Matthew, St Mark, St Luke and St John successively. Here there is a blaze of colour, with every shade of blue, green and red set off by the gold and porphyry of the architecture.

The occupation of Ravenna by Theodoric the Goth (493–526) marked a change in the style of mosaic decoration. That it quickly deteriorated when cut off from the inspiration of Constantinople is evident in the treatment of the dome mosaic of the Arian Baptistery, which is an uninspired copy of the same feature in the Baptistery of the Orthodox. In S. Apollinare Nuovo, however, where the panels above and the figures between the windows belong to Theodoric's time, the style though still different is arresting in its direct appeal. Moreover, these panels represent the first attempt to tell the story of Christ's life and Passion in a number of separate episodes, a scheme designed for the instruction of the faithful which was to dominate the decoration of churches for centuries to come. Along the northern side of the nave, in the scenes of Christ's ministry and miracles, Our Lord is portrayed as the young, beardless figure of Classical tradition; to the south, where His Passion is depicted, He is the more sombre, bearded Christ, the 'man of sorrows and acquainted with grief', whose image gradually became standard throughout the Christian world. The style, it must be admitted, is not specially distinguished, but each panel tells its story with a simple directness that takes one back to the late antique art of Rome, with its frontal figures and lack of interest in a picturesque background. Christ, the dominant personality in each scene, is of superhuman stature. The single figures of prophets and Evangelists between the windows of the clerestory are the less effective for their isolation.

During the early Christian period, Salonika in western Thrace had close ties with Constantinople, and the midfifth century mosaics in the church of St George probably reflect the contemporary art of the capital; they are also important as the earliest known to have survived in the Eastern Empire. On the vaults of the niches in the outer wall, the noncommittal decoration with birds, stylized vegetation and geometric figures is reminiscent of the art of Syria and Cilicia as it is seen reflected in S. Costanza. The lower part of the dome, however, contains a remarkable architectural composition, acting as a background to the figures of saints of the Eastern Church with their arms raised in prayer. Inevitably the airy lightness of the

Plates 72, 73

Plate 76

165

architecture recalls the Fourth Style of Pompeian painting, itself possibly derived from Alexandria. With the nearly contemporary architectural panels of the Baptistery of the Orthodox it has less in common, since the mansions of the Heavenly City in St George's have an 'other-worldly' quality that did not reach Ravenna until a century later.

While wall-mosaics of the fourth and fifth centuries are comparatively rare, a very large number of floor mosaics has survived, specially in the Near East and North Africa. Consequently, the latter can only be treated in very general terms. For obvious reasons, their decoration was restricted to subjects which could be trodden underfoot without doing violence to religious feeling, which in effect meant an embargo on all scenes or personages of the New Testament, as well as many of the Old. Thus the majority of such mosaics are not obviously Christian, and almost identical mosaics could be, and were, used indiscriminately for churches and secular buildings of all types; in fact, they were really a type of permanent, or at any rate, very durable carpet. Many are decorated exclusively with geometric patterns; others with birds and beasts, the signs of the Zodiac, the Seasons, and many other motives drawn from pagan antiquity, either dispersed over the field or enclosed in interlinking roundels, ellipses, rhombs and lozenges. The vine, growing from an amphora, which encircles animals and birds in its looping branches and tendrils is possibly suggestive of Christian allegory; but the river landscapes and hunting scenes, which are also common, are often only Christian in so far as they are not certainly pagan. Choricius of Gaza, writing on the subject, suggests that some pagan subjects should be avoided 'lest even the memory of those fables intrude upon the sacred place', but fully recom-mends 'the Nile . . . with meadows along its banks and all the various species of birds that often wash in the river's streams and dwell in the meadows'. A Nilotic scene is, of course, used

allegorically on the famous fourth-century floor of the cathedral
at Aquileia, where the *Amores* fishing represent the Christian
ministry. A popular scene in Syria and Cilicia during the
fifth century is the so-called Messianic Paradise or Peaceful
Kingdom, in which the fulfilment of Isaiah's prophecy is
portrayed, with or without the relevant text (XI, 6–8). In the
Cilician Plain, the text is faithfully followed at Karlık, and
probably also at Corycus in the western part of the province,
though the mosaic there has not yet been fully uncovered. A
rustic version of the Paradise was found at Ayaş (Elaeusa
Sebaste) near Corycus, but the arrangement of the animals is
apparently haphazard. A fifth-century floor mosaic, recently
discovered at Misis (Mopsuestia) is specially interesting. It
contains Old Testament scenes, based on the stories of Noah
and Samson, but the style of some elements of the whole work
is inconsistent, as if parts of it were entrusted to different
craftsmen. Though all the events in the life of Samson are the
work of a very competent mosaicist who worked in the
Hellenistic tradition, the animals and birds that surround
Noah's ark—a little cabinet on four legs—are drawn straight
from the pattern book. Again, the 'inhabited' acanthus scroll
work, which is used to separate different panels, is surely the
work of yet another artist with a great feeling for contrast in
depth of light and shade—a man, it might be thought, who
had often seen such scroll work executed in stone.

Plate 69

Plate 70, 71

Sculpture in the round was the art least favoured by the early
Church. For religious reasons it was abhorrent to the Jews, and
their prejudice had been inherited by the Christians who themselves had good reason to remember that their worst sufferings
had been due to their refusal to sacrifice to the statues of the
Emperors. Finally, it was the art, *par excellence*, of the old pagan
world which Christians were at such pains to discredit. The
liberation of the Church did not, however, mean the immediate
end of sculpture in the round; rather its importance gradually

167

waned, until it was almost everywhere succeeded by relief work in stone, ivory and wood. Sculpture in the round does not appear ever to have had a place in the decoration of post-Constantinian churches.

Plate 30 The colossal portrait head of Constantine the Great, now to be seen on the Capitol in Rome, is typical of its age (*c.* 312). For some time past, and particularly towards the end of the third century, sculptors had been returning to the principles governing the archaic art of Greece. For portrait busts, frontality was again the rule, and the easy transition from plane to plane was rejected in favour of a treatment almost harsh in its clear definition. Facial details were disregarded; the eyebrows were mere arched ridges, diagonally scored to indicate their texture, and the hair was summarily treated likewise. Thus illusionism was abandoned for a simple statement of fact, designed to make a single immediate impact. The portrait head of Constantine, originally part of a colossal statue which stood in the Basilica of Maxentius, is striking in its delineation of a strong and determined character. In it, although the Roman tradition of individual portraiture still lives, the means of expression are no less clearly borrowed from Oriental sources.

The drapery of full length portrait statues of the period also shows a return to the archaic convention, for its folds are not controlled by the movement or posture of the body, but follow a rigidly patterned arrangement, depending largely on 'colorism' for its effect. The statue of Julian the Apostate (361–363) is no exception in this respect, though the alert and challenging features are, perhaps not altogether accidentally, somewhat more personal and realistic than was usual at that time.

Two more works, both in Istanbul, are further evidence that good sculpture in the round was still being done in the late Plate 33 fourth and early fifth centuries. The first, a head of the young Emperor Arcadius (395–408), is a sensitive portrait, reflecting the growing refinement of Constantinopolitan art, with more than a backward glance at the Classical past; the other, the bust Plate 34 of an Evangelist, is more in the expressionist style of the Orient. The two works cannot be many decades apart, and indicate Constantinople's growing importance as a clearing house for the art of the Christian world.

Though statues in the round were made for a secular purpose, figured relief and architectural sculpture was common enough in the decoration of churches. Indeed, the early Christian worshipper, on entering a church of any importance, would very likely have passed through a sculptured doorway hung with carved wooden portals; once inside, he would have seen the pierced stonework of the *cancellus* surrounding the altar at the entrance to the sanctuary, and on one, or both sides of this, a stone ambo, or pulpit, carved in relief. In addition, the capitals of the interior order gave the sculptor great scope.

As an outstanding example of the decorative value of architectural sculpture in ecclesiastical use, the fifth-century monastery complex at Alahan in Isauria may be specially cited. The pilgrim entering the monastery complex from the west, passed through a monumental gateway into a building of basilical type which was possibly, though not certainly, a church. This gateway, still relatively undamaged, was crowned Plate 29 by a cornice decorated with crisp vine scrolls, and with crossed fish or birds substituted for the usual classical motives found between the horizontal consoles. On the underside of the lintel is a composition of which the centre-piece is a tetramorph of the four beasts of Ezekiel's vision, while the inner side of each door-post carries the full length figure of an archangel; Gabriel to the north and Michael to the south. In the centre of the western face of the lintel is a medallion containing the head of Christ, with supporting angels to either side.

The composition on the underside of the lintel block is a Fig. 31 masterpiece of religious art, in which the mystical quality of the Apocalyptic vision is admirably expressed; indeed it may be

Fig. 31 Relief sculpture on the underside of the lintel block of the main gateway leading into the monastery complex at Alahan in Isauria. The subject consists of the four beasts of Ezekiel's vision arranged as a tetramorph. Width 7 ft 2 in.; depth 2 ft 4 in. Mid fifth century

doubted whether this essentially Oriental subject has ever been treated in a way more completely acceptable to a Western mind. In the figure of the angel which centralizes the composition, of the watchful lion, of the ponderous ox, of the flying eagle which covers the junction of the other three, is a solid foundation which fully emphasizes the fine sweep of the wings to which the viewer's attention is inevitably drawn. The effect is of immense power sustained by a transcendental inner life.

Plate 28   The reliefs of SS. Michael and Gabriel on the inner surfaces of the door-posts are less spectacular than the tetramorph and owing to their exposed position are more weathered. They are, however, noteworthy both technically and iconographically. At first glance there is a superficial resemblance in pose and attributes to the sixth-century ivory of St Michael in the British Museum. The Alahan sculpture lacks the finesse of the ivory, and represents rather the surrender of Hellenistic naturalism to impulses from Syria and lands farther east. Indeed, the sculptor, in cutting the figures sharply from their background, so that they almost resemble silhouettes, displays far less interest in modelling than in the case of the tetramorph, and his con-ception of form here seems confined to two dimensions. It is the niche, with its utter disregard of spatial illusionism, which most suggests the influence of the east. The two acanthus capitals are suspended in space with no supporting columns below them. As capitals they are quite unsubstantial, and the acanthus leaves, of which they are composed, are treated solely as stylized ornament with barely a reminiscence of the vegetable forms from which they are ultimately derived.

The reliefs on the southern door of the monastery church itself are equally arresting. On the outer faces of the jambs and lintel is a vine scroll with birds pecking at the grape clusters, while the inner surfaces are carved with a brilliant composition of fish, the old Christian symbol here exploited to the full. Curiously, the central door has, in the same relative positions, a composition based on the pagan cornucopia.

Inside the church, the majority of column capitals are of an orthodox, though uninspired Corinthian type; four, however, have flying eagles substituted for the normal angle volutes. This tendency towards the baroque was no innovation in south-eastern Asia Minor, and the colonnaded street at Pompeiopolis in Cilicia contains many examples of unusual capitals. On some, the acanthus leaves swirl, as if swept by the wind, while in others human figures, busts and, again, flying eagles take the place of angle volutes. At Hieropolis Castabala in the Cilician Plain, an otherwise normal Corinthian capital in a fifth-century basilica has a peacock (?) in place of the central volutes. In Constantinople, there are numerous varieties of the baroque capital, one of which, decorated with a head whose hair and beard are made of acanthus leaves, recalls a not uncommon pagan motif, also found in the Great Palace of the Byzantine Emperors. Another, with four winged horses at the angles is reminiscent of Achaemenid art. Generally, however, and specially in the first Golden Age, Constantinople favoured the 'basket' capital, in which the acanthus decoration is purely vestigial, and rather intended as a suitable medium for a fully 'coloristic' treatment.

Plate 27

Fig. 32

Plate 22

Plate 23

Plate 25

Plate 24

The ambo, probably a direct loan from the Jewish Synagogue, was an important item of church furniture. In a simple form, as found in 1959 in the church without the walls at Dağ Pazarı (Coropissus?) in Isauria, it consisted of a circular stone plat/ form with a wooden balustrade. In larger churches, the ambo was often completely of stone or marble, with a flight of steps leading up to a pulpit/like structure, and of this type examples exist at Lepcis Magna in Tripolitania and, reconstructed, in the church of S. Apollinare Nuovo in Ravenna. Perhaps the most elaborate, however, is the fragmentary ambo in Istanbul, to be dated to the fifth century. The reading platform was again reached by steps, but it is the lower portion, or podium, that is of special interest. To the right of the steps the Shepherds pay homage to the Madonna and Child; on the left, the Magi come up with their gifts. In common with some Anatolian sarco/ phagi of slightly earlier date, the whole surface is arranged in a series of niches, each containing a figure in high relief. The frontal group of the Madonna and Child, the 'coloristic' treat/ ment of the vine and acanthus scroll above the figures, are strongly suggestive of the Syrian style that penetrated Cilicia in the same period. Indeed, the sculpture of this ambo and of a contemporary podium in the monastery church at Alahan is strikingly similar, though at Alahan the conch/headed niches contain only simple crosses in relief.

The richest field for Christian relief sculpture is provided by the sarcophagi which, even before Constantine, had a con/ siderable tradition behind them. After the Peace of the Church, with ambiguity no longer necessary, first the life and miracles

Fig. 32   Decorative panel of fish in relief on the south door of the monastery/church at Alahan in Isauria. Height 6 ft 1½ in.; width 10 in. Mid fifth century

of Christ and, later, His passion were all freely portrayed. Narrative pure and simple was also gradually replaced by an emphasis on Christian dogma, and New Testament scenes were paired with the episodes from the Old Testament that prefigured them. In Rome, the earliest fourth-century frieze sarcophagi are very close in style to the relief sculptures on the Arch of Constantine, erected probably not long after the Battle of the Milvian Bridge. Indeed, the scene of the destruction of Maxentius and his army in the Tiber on the southern side of the Arch might well be thought a prototype for the many sarcophagi in Rome and southern Gaul which illustrate Pharaoh and his Egyptians being engulfed in the Red Sea. Other friezes on the Arch exemplify the tendency of Roman sculptors to adopt the formal approach which characterized contemporary works of sculpture in the round. The figures are squat, often frontal, and arranged almost mechanically, in symmetrical, or near symmetrical groups. Two reliefs on the northern side of the Arch illustrate the trend; one shows the Emperor standing on the Rostra in the Forum and addressing the People of Rome (*allocutio*), the other is a scene of the distribution of largesse and favours to chosen citizens (*congiarium*). The latter is in two registers, as it is intended to show the interior of a two-storeyed building. The Emperor is seated on his throne, in a similar posture to that so often taken by Christ (e.g. on the Milan and Adana reliquaries).

Plate 32

The reliefs on the base of the Obelisk of Theodosius (*c.* 390) in the At Meydanı (the Hippodrome) in Istanbul, represent a further development from this style, and the figures are now almost two-dimensional. The scenes on the north and south sides, of Theodosius presiding at the games and presenting a wreath to a victor respectively, strictly observe the law of frontality, and no concession is made to reality. The balustrade in front of the Imperial box is not unlike the *cancellus* in a church. These reliefs mark the *ne plus ultra* of this particular

Plate 31

style, and such work is not found even on contemporary sarcophagi, either from Asia or the West. The influence of the friezes on Constantine's Arch is quite apparent, however, in some Roman examples, of which both the lid and the case were normally carved in high relief.

A feature of the frieze sarcophagus is the way in which the same biblical events are repeated time and again to emphasize a simple article of faith, while portrait busts of the dead, enclosed in a plain or scalloped roundel, are inserted in the centre, or at the sides of the frieze. A single pagan scene is included in some of the earlier examples. A most interesting sarcophagus of this group is that of Claudianus (mid fourth century) in the Museo delle Terme in Rome. On the lid, left of the central inscription, are the Nativity, the Sacrifice of Isaac, and Moses receiving the tables on Sinai, symbolizing the Redemption and the institution of the new law by Christ. On the right, the scene of *Amores* gathering in the harvest is a likely allusion to Luke x, 2. On the case, the same message of the Redemption is conveyed, though the symbolism is confused in its arrangement. In the centre, the female *orans* represents the soul of the deceased. On either side of her, the miracles of Christ and the cycle of St Peter (his denial of Our Lord, his arrest, and the symbolic striking of water from the rock) are not obviously grouped in any logical order; on the other hand, they are exactly repeated in the lower frieze of the sarcophagus of Sabinus in the same museum, and the order may have had a significance which is now lost. The message is far clearer in the contemporary sarcophagus of a husband and wife in the Lateran Museum. On the upper frieze, the creation of man by the three persons of the Trinity is followed by the Fall, both scenes on the left of the central medallion containing the busts of the deceased. On the right, the miracles of Cana and the Multiplication, followed by the raising of Lazarus, symbolize the deliverance of man and his hope of eternal life. In the lower register, the Adoration of

Plate 37

the Magi and the healing of the man born blind are balanced by the St Peter cycle. In the centre, as the symbol of deliverance, stands Daniel between two lions. In the Terme Museum, another frieze sarcophagus contains a scene of the Entry into Jerusalem on the first Palm Sunday. Typically, the Roman sculptor represented the scene in the full detail of St Matthew's narrative (xxi, 1–2), with the colt running beside the ass ridden by Our Lord.

Plate 40

Later in the fourth century, a new type of sarcophagus evolved, which seems certainly to have been of Asiatic origin. This is the niched columnar type, in which single figures or groups which are fundamentally related are divided from each other by colonnettes. The type-specimen usually cited is the fragmentary sarcophagus from Sidamara, now in Berlin, in which Christ and His Apostles are so arranged. However, its origins go back beyond the fourth century, and Ghandaran reliefs, themselves derived from Hellenistic sources, show almost the same treatment. A recently discovered sarcophagus at Balabolu (Adrassus ?) in Isauria may also prove to be a pagan prototype, though it cannot probably be much earlier than the turn of the third and fourth centuries. The theme of the relief is clearly secular, and seems to commemorate some warlike episode. The two seated figures at either end must be the commanders of opposing armies, of which the one on the left, his foot resting on a captured fortress, is the victor. Two soldiers lead a bound captive before him. The action is barely interrupted by the arcades which separate the figures.

Plate 42

Despite its eastern origin, the columnar niched sarcophagus is most often found in Italy and southern Gaul. The decoration is fairly consistent within a limited range of subjects, of which the commonest is perhaps the central Christ, as Teacher or Law-giver, flanked more or less symmetrically by the Apostles. Sometimes the place of Our Lord is taken by an *orans*, with scenes of Christ's miracles on either side, while another

Plate 38

Plate 39

effective composition consists of the wreathed *labarum*, the standard of Constantine now symbolic of the triumph of Christ's death and resurrection, flanked by episodes from the Passion. Sometimes elements from all three are combined. A fine example in the Vatican is a marble sarcophagus with an elaborate Corinthian colonnade, which divides the surface into seven niches. In the centre, Our Lord, enthroned above the vault of Heaven (here personalized as a young, beardless deity), presents the New Law to St Peter, while St Paul advances from the right. At the ends are balancing scenes of Christ before Pilate and the Sacrifice of Isaac. The masterpiece among niched sarcophagi is in the Lateran Museum. Here there are five niches flanked by spirally fluted colonnettes. In the centre, a wreathed chi-rho soaring above the Cross symbolizes the resurrection, while on either side, below it, the Roman guardians of the tomb idle or sleep. The four side niches are devoted to scenes from the Passion. On the right, Our Lord, an authoritative figure for all that He is under guard, confronts Pilate, who turns aside in confusion from the bowl and ewer of water, unable to meet His eye; on the left, the Crowning with Thorns and Simon of Cyrene carrying the cross complete the composition. The decoration of this sarco‚ phagus seems to reflect the faith of the dead man himself in his triumph over the grave, for even the scenes of the Passion are crowned by wreaths of victory. In the south of France, a colonnade of trees sometimes takes the place of the usual architectural features, a scheme known as far east as Ghandara.

Another specialized group of sarcophagi, probably inspired by late Hellenistic art, is known as the 'city gate' type, in which biblical scenes are portrayed against a continuous architectural background, though without historical sequence. A fine example of one such, in which the delicacy of the relief recalls an ivory carving, is in the Lateran Museum. True, the icono‚ graphic detail is inconsistent; Our Lord, confronting St Peter after his denial, is young and beardless, and yet is fully bearded in the scene of the healing of the woman with the issue of blood. On the other hand, the realism of the architectural background, with its walls, basilica and baptistery (?) almost suggests the features of a real city. Another 'city-gate' sarco-phagus, below the ambo of S. Ambrogio in Milan, shows Christ enthroned between the Apostles, against a more fanciful background of turrets and crenellated arches.

Many of the 'city gate' and columnar niched sarcophagi have been attributed to Eastern craftsmen working in the ateliers of southern Gaul, and some made of Proconnesan marble were, no doubt, imported. The drill was freely used to produce a 'coloristic' effect, e.g. the niched sarcopagus in Arles (Musée chrétien lapidaire, No. 17) where Christ is seen entrusting St Peter with the new law. Marion Lawrence describes Rome in the fourth and fifth centuries as 'a backwater', yet the high quality of the work found there is in sharp contrast with the generally cruder standards of southern Gaul, and it is hard to believe in Provençal inspiration for the Roman works mentioned above.

The Christian strigillated sarcophagus (so called from the resemblance of the S-shaped flutes on its surface to the strigils, or oil-scrapers used in gymnasia) represents an old decorative style brought up to date, and such details of arrangement as the central roundel and panels or figures at either end are taken over direct from pagan prototypes.

The Ravennate collection, which comprises a small group of sarcophagi of the late fifth and early sixth centuries, apparently owes nothing either to Rome or to the East as such. In fact, the use of decorative symbolism or of figured scenes in the Neo-Attic style suggests the influence of Constantinople. The Constantinian *labarum*, with or without a wreath, is frequently used on the curved lids, and on one example in S. Apollinare in Classe, the whole side is decorated with vine scrolls and confronted peacocks. Figured scenes, like the Adoration of the Magi or the *Traditio Legis*, are portrayed without architectural or other background; parallel works from Constantinople are a sarcophagus in the Istanbul Museum, where the long side is decorated with two angles supporting a wreathed chi-rho, and a fragmentary relief from Bakırköy.

Plate 41

Carved ivory panels, whether as devotional objects, like icons, or as separate parts of larger works, were produced in all the main Christian centres, and many can be placed satisfactorily on stylistic grounds alone. Nevertheless, being easily portable, their provenance is not always clear, and there are few pieces whose origin and date are not disputed. The securely dated Consular Diptychs form an obvious exception, and are most useful as comparative evidence. Each leaf is normally carved with a portrait of the Consul, full length or enthroned, and this arrangement is copied in other secular diptychs, like that of Stilicho with his wife and child at Monza, or the fifth-century Vienna diptych of Rome and Con-stantinople. In a religious context, it appears in the single leaf figuring the archangel Michael in the British Museum. There is no hard and fast rule, however, and the decorative scheme of

Plates 59, 60

the famous ivory diptych in the Bargello Museum in Florence is quite different. One leaf is used for one complete picture, of Adam comfortably reclining beside an oak tree in Eden with all the animal creation at his feet. On the other leaf, episodes from the life of St Paul are depicted in sequence, one below the other. The Apostle, easily recognizable in Christian icono-graphy by his receding hair and long pointed beard, is first shown teaching, or disputing with an elderly man. Below, St Paul is seen in Malta, after his shipwreck, shaking the viper from his hand into the fire, to the amazement of the bystanders, amongst whom is Publius, later his host, whose father St Paul cured of a wasting disease. At the bottom, Publius' father and another invalid with a withered arm are depicted. The style of this diptych, which is probably of fifth-century date, is in the Classical tradition, and despite the frequency of the Paradise theme in East Christian iconography, its provenance cannot be settled on this criterion alone. Constantinople has been suggested by Delbrueck and Talbot Rice, and the Neo-Attic style of the St Paul leaf would seem to support the conjecture.

Another group of ivories consists of small *pyxides*, or lidded boxes, many of which are round, being carved from a single section of tusk. Those produced for the secular market and probably intended for trinkets and cosmetics are recognizable by their decoration with scenes from pagan mythology. The majority, however, with religious decoration, probably housed small objects of piety or relics. Not surprisingly, the icono-graphy runs parallel with that of sculptured sarcophagi, and most of them date between the fourth and sixth centuries. The main centres of production seem to have been Alexandria, Antioch, Constantinople, Rome, northern Italy and southern Gaul. More elaborate boxes were also made of several panels of ivory, and of these the finest is the so-called Lipsanotheca at Brescia, probably a late fourth-century work which originated in the north of Italy, probably at Milan. The Lipsanotheca, which is the work of a single master, is an oblong box with a lid. All the surfaces are richly carved, and the decoration forms a unique compendium of Christian iconography as known at that time. On the lid, episodes from Our Lord's Passion, from the Agony in the Garden to His Condemnation by Pilate are represented in the continuous style; on the side and end panels, each of which is divided into three registers, are scenes from the Old and New Testaments. Round the lower part of the lid are medallions containing the heads of Apostles and Saints. The Lipsanotheca master was a consummate artist, notable for an unerring sense of composition and meticulous attention to detail, and though there are upwards of a hundred figures all told, no scene appears crowded. There is also a deliberate

Plate 54

contrast in the treatment of different scenes. Thus, on the lid, the drama of the Passion unfolds in quiet dignity, while on the lower zones of the long sides, the story of Susanna and the Elders and of David and Goliath are told with an obvious interest in the factual narration of the action. It is this quality of realism attached to a pure Neo-Attic style that suggests Milan as the place of its manufacture. The decoration of four panels of an early fifth-century ivory casket in the British Museum again displays a pronounced interest in the narrative and factual element; but the coarser treatment and the dumpy proportions of the figures suggest the influence of a centre less sophisticated than Milan, and southern Gaul seems likely. The scenes are all from the Passion cycle, beginning in the Judg-ment Hall of Pilate and ending with the Incredulity of St Thomas. Most important, however, is the first known factual portrayal of the Crucifixion in all its stark realism. The artist is greatly concerned for detail, as is clear from his treatment of the Denial of St Peter, where the Apostle is seen warming his hands at the brazier in the court of Caiaphas, and in the Crucifixion panel, where thirty pieces of silver spill from an open bag below the hanging figure of Judas. For a study of the Eastern schools of ivory carving, perhaps the best example is the Throne of Maximian in Ravenna, which is described in the next chapter.

With the notable exception of the door panels of S. Sabina in Rome (*c.* 432), very little remains of early Christian carving in wood. The scenes portrayed chiefly belong to the usual cycle of incidents in Christ's life, His miracles and those Old Testa-ment events which prefigured them. One panel contains the first representation of Our Lord crucified between the two thieves, but the scene lacks realism, as the artist could have had no first-hand knowledge of that form of execution. The iconography of the Crucifixion, as it is now familiarly known in the West, really developed in the Orient, though there in the

Plate 53

Plates 55, 56, 57, 58

Plate 56

Plate 65

Plate 66

b

c

d

e

a

Fig. 33 (a) Bronze thurible with hexagonal bowl
from Dağ Pazarı (Coropissus?) in Isauria. Total
height c. 3 ft; height of bowl c. 4 in. Round the
bowl a continuous inscription reads: 'In fulfilment
of the vow of Theodorus.' Each panel contains a
single figure: (b) adorant angel, (c) Christ, (d)
adorant angel, (e) monk with lamp and codex,
(f) monk with quill, (g) monk with a lamp and
open codex

f

g

earliest examples the figure of Christ is normally draped in a long garment (*colobium*).

Small portable objects of church furniture were often made of metal. Those in everyday use, such as lamps and thuribles, were usually of bronze, while items of church plate (e.g. the Antioch chalice) were of silver or gold. Silver was normally used for reliquary boxes. Though glass lamps are very rarely found intact, excavations often disclose the bronze chains from which they were suspended by loops in the upper rim. A common form of fifth-century lamp-chain in the East consists of a hook, a cross, and then a ring from which three smaller chains depend. Clay or metal lamps were sometimes raised on small, spirally fluted holders like large candlesticks (e.g. on the Misis Noah's Ark mosaic and on the Brescia Lipsanotheca).

Most early thuribles have been discovered in the Christian East, as a result of excavations in churches ruined soon after the Moslem invasions. The bowl, which may be rounded or hexagonal, stands on a single moulded base or on three small feet, and is usually suspended in the same way as the glass lamps, i.e. with three loops spaced round the rim for the attachment of chains. A thurible in the Adana Museum, which recently came to light at Dağ Pazarı in Isauria, is remarkable for a number of reasons. It is not only perfectly preserved and the first example of its kind from Isauria; it may also be the earliest thurible known, for it can hardly be later than the mid-fifth century. The hexagonal bowl is divided into six arcaded niches, flanked by spirally fluted Corinthian colonnettes, an arrangement recalling the columnar niched sarcophagi of Asia Minor. The focal point of the object is the niche containing the bearded figure of Christ, wearing a halo, His right hand raised in blessing and the left holding a lamp; to either side of Him an angel bends low in adoration, while each of the other three niches is filled by a saint, or a monk, warmly dressed with a cowl over his head. Two of them hold

Plate 49

lamps, and the third a *codex*. The squat dumpy figures with their large heads and enveloping drapery suggest that the thurible is of local workmanship. Indeed, some of the figures on the Adana reliquary, discovered in the same general area, afford a distinct, if more elegant parallel.

Plates 47, 48

Fig. 34 Silver spoon from the hoard found on Traprain Law in East Lothian. The bowl is inscribed with a chi-rho monogram. Total length, with bowl, 11 in. Fourth century

Of early Christian plate before Justinian, the Antioch chalice (*c.* 400) with its intricate vine motives and figures is perhaps the richest treasure. Less well known, but extremely interesting, are the fourth-century silver gilt flasks and spoons from the hoard found on Traprain Law in East Lothian. One flask, possibly an altar cruet, is decorated in repoussé, with the Fall of Man and the Adoration of the Magi, the latter appearing for the first time on metal work. Some spoons, whose bowls were adorned with the chi-rho, may well have been used for holy oil or for some other liturgical purpose.

Plates 50, 51

The majority of silver reliquaries still extant usually owe their survival to having been hidden away under the altar in the first place, and so less easily found by looters. They are normally small caskets of rectangular or oval shape, though a recently discovered example from Çırga in Isauria is like a miniature Ravennate sarcophagus. One of the largest and finest of all is the silver gilt reliquary, found below the high altar of S. Nazaro in Milan, which is decorated with scenes

Plate 45

from the Old and New Testaments. The style of this fourth-century work is Neo-Attic, but the factual treatment points to its having been manufactured in Italy, probably in Milan itself. The side on which Christ is seen enthroned amongst His Apostles is interesting for its obvious debt to secular represen-

Plates, 46, 47, 48 tations of the Emperor and his Court. The Çırga reliquary, found in 1957 and now in the Adana Museum, is in a different tradition; for although the internal evidence of an inscription places it in the second half of the fifth century, it has many primitive features. On the front, a central medallion containing

Plate 47 Christ Pantocrator is flanked by two upright panels, each containing a single male *orans* who is identified as St Conon.

Plate 48 On the back, a similar medallion, with two saints (SS. Peter and Paul ?) confronting each other across the Lamb of God, is flanked on either side by a female *orans*, to be identified with the Virgin, St Ia, or an unknown saint, according to the reading of the inscription. The two lions that accompany the figure suggest that memories of Cybele and her lion attendants were still strong in this area which, in pagan times, had been devoted to her cult.

By no means all the silver work produced in our period was destined for religious use, and a quantity of table ware and household objects has survived, notably in hoards found all over the early Christian world, from Britain to the Crimea. Naturally enough, such objects of luxury were beyond reach of any but the rich, and their decoration, like that of the secular ivory *pyxides* described above, shows how strong was the hold of the pagan classical tradition on the older and

Plate 52 wealthier Christian families. A large silver gilt casket, found in a hoard on the Esquiline Hill in Rome and now in the British Museum, may be dated to the fourth century. An inscription shows that it belonged to Proiecta, married to one Secundus, and that both were Christians. The casket, probably used for Proiecta's jewellery, must have been presented to her on her marriage, as the front is decorated (rather in the manner of a columnar niched sarcophagus) with the figure of the bride seated at her toilet and attended by two maids, a scene familiar from the time of the late red-figure Attic *pyxides* of the end of the fifth century B.C. On the back, Proiecta is seen making her way to her husband's home, while on the lid, Venus, attended by Tritons and *Amores*, reclines in a sea-shell and arranges her hair. Of Christianity there is no trace, except for the inscription, 'Proiecta and Secundus, may you live in Christ'.

There is perhaps no religion which so much emphasizes the personal relationship between God and man as does Christianity. Moreover, since man, unlike the angels, is not a pure spirit, but consists of an immortal soul and a body which shares in its resurrection, Christian memorials have always tended to perpetuate the memory of the dead in their own human likeness. This practice may be seen in the portrait heads and busts on many of the fourth-century frieze sarcophagi, of which a very fine example in the Syracuse Museum portrays a man and wife facing each other, extremely touching in their youth and freshness.

Plate 63

Another rich field for early Christian portraiture exists in the minor art of gold-glass, of which a large quantity has been found in Italy, particularly in the Catacombs. This technique, which was chiefly practised between the fourth and fifth centuries, was normally confined to the bases of drinking vessels and bowls, whereby engravings on gold leaf were com-pressed between two layers of glass. Many of the subjects were those normal to the Christian iconography of the period, and included scenes from the Old and New Testaments. Perhaps the most striking, however, are those which portrayed in-dividuals or families of every station of life, and which give us a glimpse of the men, women and children who formed the congregation of the churches already described. Rightly the most famous of all is the medallion, set into a Byzantine cross

Plate 62

of a mother with her son and daughter. These aristocratic portraits strongly resemble paintings done on second-century mummy cases at Fayyum in Egypt, and may well be the work of an Alexandrian craftsman. At the other end of the social scale is the charming family on a gold-glass base in the Vatican, where the rather smug little boy in his 'Sunday best' is the image

Plate 61 of his father. Another base, in the British Museum, is more obviously Christian, with a youthful Christ placing garlands on the heads of a middle-aged and rather angular husband and wife.

Practical archaeology is a scientific exercise. Its purpose, on the other hand, is to reveal humanity in all its aspects. And if it cannot be claimed that individual portraits of men and women long dead have more to tell us than the remains of their possessions, they do at all events provide a bridge across the gap that separates their time from ours, and perhaps helps us a little to see their world through their own undimmed eyes.

CHAPTER VIII

Justinian, Theodora, and the Golden Age

THE FIRST GOLDEN AGE of Byzantium coincided with the reign of Justinian and his consort Theodora, one of the few married couples in history to set their seal on an era. And if this age, more than most, is marked by the almost living personalities of its leading figures, is it altogether fanciful to suppose that this is partly so because their features are so familiar? For fourteen centuries the mosaic portraits of Justinian and Theodora have faced each other across the apse of S. Vitale at Ravenna, and there they both, in a sense, still live, separated from the modern world in time alone, in that indirect yet almost intimate relationship with the viewer of today that characterizes the appearance of the Sovereign on the balcony at Buckingham Palace to the crowd at the gates. Justinian, with his blunt, uncompromising, rather swarthy features and thinning hair; Theodora, svelte, intense and self-possessed— few portraits, even including Holbein's Henry the Eighth, the very embodiment of a new and vulgar England—so success/ fully project the personalities of their subjects across the centuries.

The civilization of sixth-century Byzantium was, above all, Christian, and since neither before nor since has so complete an amalgam of European and Oriental traditions been possible, its art has a transcendental quality that alone fully expresses the material catholicity of the Christian heritage. Within little more than a century, although Byzantine relations with Western Europe were not completely severed, the new nations in process of formation there had little or nothing to contribute, while in the East, Syria and Egypt were lost to Islam, and so the great centres of Alexandria and Antioch ceased to play any distinctive role. In the half century or so that is spanned by the period of Justinian's power, however, churches were built and decorated with a degree of excellence that has since rarely been approached, let alone surpassed.

Just as sculpture and painting were the major arts of the Classical world, so the Byzantine spirit was most perfectly manifested in the art of mosaic. It was entirely suited to the end for which it was primarily intended, the decoration of church interiors, where the ever-changing contrast of bright light and deep shade on arch, vault and dome threw out a fresh challenge to the artist, a challenge which the painter, most at home in the adornment of the flat, evenly lighted surface, could never have met with equal success. The Byzantine mosaicist, unlike the painter, could vary the material texture of his work, and by the skilful management of his *tesserae*, now set flush with the wall, now projecting and now receding, could call into being shadows and highlights that neutralized curved surfaces in the light of day. Against the glow of lamps and candles, in the evening, the same mosaic would have glanced and glittered like some jewelled brocade. Of its nature, however, mosaic is a limited, and at the same time a limiting, medium, and is consequently, in the present writer's view, at its best where it does not try to imitate painting, especially of the narrative or highly naturalistic variety. For all its merit, the Alexander mosaic from Pompeii is no real compensation for the lost masterpiece of Philoxenus of Eretria. Equally true is it that the subjects of the mosaics in S. Vitale, S. Apollinare Nuovo or S. Apollinare in Classe could never have been so successful in the medium of painting.

In the architectural sculpture of the great churches of the First Golden Age, the same preoccupation with exploiting the variations of intensity in light and shade is equally apparent, especially in the treatment of column capitals and imposts or, for example, of the fretted stone balustrades and sculptured orthostats that separated the chancel from the rest of the church.

The sculptured ambo, or pulpit, from Salonika, and now in   Plate 43
Istanbul, is also an important representative of this 'coloristic'
style. For the rest, on wall panels and floors, the use of variously
coloured marbles in bold geometric patterns again emphasized
the love of magnificence, achieved by striking contrasts, that
marked the beginnings of the new style.

For all that is truly representative of Byzantine art in the First
Golden Age, one need look no further than the churches, of
which the Emperor, as vice-gerent of God on earth, was the
supreme patron and benefactor. Of those which still stand,
S. Sophia in Constantinople and S. Vitale in Ravenna are
exceptional for their architecture and mosaics, and in this
chapter these monuments alone are described in some detail.
It must not be forgotten, however, that the church of SS.
Sergius and Bacchus in Constantinople is of great importance
architecturally as a near contemporary of S. Vitale, and that
in the basilicas dedicated to S. Apollinare in Ravenna and in
Classe, a few miles south of the city, are exceptionally fine
mosaics of more or less the same period.

Fig. 35   Church of S. Vitale at Ravenna.
Basic plan is an octagon within an octagon,
with a dome rising from squinches. 530–47

0   5   10   15   20

metres

189

The plan of S. Vitale is an octagon within an octagon, with a polygonal apse projecting from the eastern perimeter. The inner space, defined by eight wedge-shaped piers, supports an octagonal drum from which, by means of squinches, rises a light dome constructed of interlinking terra-cotta pipes. Between each pair of piers is a two-storeyed columnar *exedra*, of which the upper one is roofed by a semi-dome. These *exedrae* equally give access to the upper and lower cross vaulted ambulatories which, with the exception of the eastern side, run round the whole building. At first sight, S. Vitale appears to have been built for strength, with the *exedrae* playing their part in absorbing the outward thrust of the dome; closer inspection, however, reveals that the massive piers supporting the drum are reinforced by radial walls which project from the outside of the building, and are in combination quite strong enough to perform their function without the further aid of niche buttressing in the form of *exedrae*.

It has already been shown that there are some grounds for believing that the architecture of S. Vitale is explicable in terms of a continuous and developing tradition first in Rome, and later in North Italy, and that in this connexion the church of S. Lorenzo in Milan is of capital importance. Even so, the *exedrae* appear as an intrusive feature, possibly from the Hellenistic litoral of Syria, and it would be most unwise to consider the 'Italian' thesis as proven for S. Vitale without due consideration of the church of SS. Sergius and Bacchus in Constantinople. Here, as Ward-Perkins has pointed out, a most important element in the discussion is the time factor, since to prove direct Byzantine influence on S. Vitale, it would be most useful to show that SS. Sergius and Bacchus was the earlier building. In fact, this is rather doubtful, since S. Vitale had been founded during the episcopate of Ecclesius, which began in 522 and ended in 534 at the latest, while Ravenna was still under Gothic domination. Between 524 and

526 Ecclesius visited Constantinople, at which time it is unlikely that he would have seen SS. Sergius and Bacchus, since in that church the column capitals bear the monograms of Justinian and Theodora, who only succeeded to the Empire in 527. The use of squinches to effect the transition from an octagon to the dome in S. Vitale is not specially relevant, since although squinches probably originated in the East, their occurrence in the Baptistery of Soter in Naples shows that they were known in Italy half a century before the foundation of S. Vitale. By the nature of its mosaics and the treatment of its architectural sculpture, the general impression given by S. Vitale is overwhelmingly that of a Byzantine monument. Even so, the decoration can, and should be considered outside its architectural context.

The chancel of S. Vitale presents the viewer with a series of unrivalled mosaics of the Justinianic period. The earliest perhaps is that in the conch of the apse, since it includes the figure of the Bishop Ecclesius, who founded the church. In the centre is Christ, enthroned on the orb of the world and flanked by angels. On His right, S. Vitale receives his martyr's crown, while on the left Ecclesius offers Him a model of the new church. The young and beardless Christ, like the Good Shepherd in the Mausoleum of Galla Placidia, is in the Hellenistic tradition, but for all its youth the figure is one of great authority and majesty. Moreover, the picturesque back/ground of verdure and flowers, through which flow the four rivers of Paradise, is not so much a setting—as it is in the Mausoleum—as an attribute of the powerful figures that dominate the composition. To either side of the altar, events from the Old Testament symbolic of the Sacrifice of Calvary and the Eucharistic meal are depicted. On the south side stand Abel and Melchisidech, one on either side of the sacrificial altar, while to the north the composite scene is of Abraham and Sarah entertaining the three angels under the shade of a great

Plate 77

Plate 68

Plates 72, 73 tree, and the Sacrifice of Isaac. Unlike the earlier scenes of Our Lord's life and Passion in S. Apollinare Nuovo which are sober and factual (thus perhaps representing the survival of the Roman tradition), and which in any case have a didactic purpose, these mosaics in S. Vitale have an elaboration and fluency which, combined with a natural or architectural back, ground, is still reminiscent of the picturesque style of Alexandria.

The two panels which contain the portraits of Justinian and Theodora are probably the latest of the mosaics in the church, and may date to the year of its consecration in 547. In any case they have a character which sets them apart from the rest, and it may well be, as Laurent suggested, that they commemorate the participation of the Emperor and his wife at the actual ceremony of consecration. On the south side, the composition is dominated by Justinian and the austere figure of Bishop Maximian (546–553) who leads the way into the sanctuary, a jewelled cross in his right hand. The Bishop is attended by two deacons, one holding a book, the other a thurible with three feet and suspended from three chains, like the fifth-century example from Dağ Pazarı in Isauria. With the Emperor are two of his retinue and some members of the household guard.

Plate 78 To the north, Theodora is seen just outside the church, the knotted curtain at the door—so familiar still in Greece and the Near East—held back by a court official to allow her to pass. Behind her follow the ladies of her retinue, each one gorgeously dressed and immaculately coiffed. Theodora herself, even more resplendent with jewels than her husband, wears a purple chlamys with the Adoration of the Magi richly embroidered above the hem. The style of these two masterpieces is at first baffling in its apparent contradictions, for the air of realism is largely achieved by unrealistic means. In the first place, the figures do not tread the ground firmly, but rather appear to float just above it; in the second, the fall of the sumptuous drapery in heavy parallel folds, is barely affected by the posture of the persons that it clothes, but seemingly exists in its own right as an exercise in the organization of colour and design. The paradox is completed by the outstanding portraiture, which transforms so many potential lay-figures into separate personages with individual characters and idiosyncrasies. Our attention is not monopolized by Justinian and Theodora, nor even by Maximian. All the rest play their part, not least the last lady in Theodora's retinue, whose attention has wandered from the solemn ceremony at which she is so soon to be present.

Since the Justinian and Theodora panels may fairly be described as the first known representatives of a fully developed Byzantine style, it is fruitless to search for contemporary parallels. Nevertheless, they conjure up ghosts from the past, from such works as the processional frieze of the Ara Pacis Augustae at Rome, which is in the full classical tradition, to the Sacrifice of Conon in the Temple of the Palmyrene gods at Dura on the Euphrates. To the West is due the individuality of the portraiture and the sense of historical occasion; to the East, the frontality of the figures, the elaboration of the drapery and, above all, the transcendental quality of the work and its direct emotional appeal.

In the basilica of S. Apollinare Nuovo, where the mosaic panels produced under the patronage of Theodoric have already been described, the face of the walls immediately above the arcades was filled with two processions of martyrs, both men and women. On the north side, preceded by the Three Kings, the women advance towards the enthroned Madonna and Child with their retinue of angels, while on the south a similar procession of men—each holding in his right hand, as the women do, his martyr's crown—moves towards Christ Him-self. These mosaics, probably dating to about 568, are uniquely beautiful, particularly the northern procession. The back-ground is of gold, and behind the magnificent, urgent figures of the Magi the women move rhythmically and slow, past a landscape of palm-trees growing from emerald green grass in which bloom brightly coloured flowers and shrubs. The movement of each woman towards the Virgin is expressed by the direction of her body, though each seems momentarily to have paused. Though their faces are turned towards the viewer, the expression is withdrawn and remote; they have no part in our world, nor we in theirs. The frontal figures of the Madonna and her attendant angels, the rich colour and sumptuous dress of the Magi and the procession behind them, the picturesque background—all these are of the East. Only the arrangement of a rhythmic progress towards a supernatural goal and the absence of a limiting time factor inevitably recall another procession, that of the Parthenon frieze, executed under Pheidias' direction a full millennium before. On the south side, the men's procession sets out from a spacious building, labelled PALATIUM, a conventionalized representation of Theodoric's Palace at Ravenna.

Plate 74

The mosaics of S. Apollinare in Classe display another facet of the Byzantine style in the First Golden Age, for this time it is the picturesque element that predominates in the conch of the apse where the patron saint stands, arms outstretched in prayer, with the twelve Apostles, represented as sheep, on either side of him. In the processional scenes of S. Apollinare Nuovo the background is an adjunct, however beautiful, to the all-important human figures; here its role is grander, and harks back to the Paradise of pre-Constantinian times. Full of ancient memories too is the superb symbolism of the Transfiguration which occupies the upper zone of the conch. Here a jewelled cross against a turquoise sky studded with golden stars represents the transfigured Christ, while three sheep—the Apostles Peter, James and John—look up in awe. On the upper register of the triumphal arch are the four Evangelists, depicted as the beasts of Ezekiel's vision, attendant upon Christ, while below, issuing from tall buildings which represent the cities of

Bethlehem and Jerusalem, are the twelve Apostles, again in the guise of sheep. The coloured clouds that float in turquoise and golden skies recall those of the apse mosaic in S. Vitale.

Across the Adriatic, in the basilical church at Parenzo in Istria, the mosaics, which are of Justinian's period, are of lower quality, and the treatment is somewhat mechanical and wooden. However, it has a claim to distinction, as a group of the Madonna and Child occurs here for the first time in the conch of the apse, which was later to be her canonical setting, just as was the dome for the figure of Christ Pantocrator.

It is reported that Justinian, when he entered the completed church of the Divine Wisdom which he had founded at Constantinople, gave thanks to God for allowing him thereby to surpass the glory of Solomon. Fourteen centuries later, St Sophia, though nowadays thinly disguised as a museum, remains the most breathtaking monument of Christendom. Moreover, it is not modern taste that has placed it at this pinnacle of renown; from the beginning, contemporary writers praised its architectural splendour, and in particular the great dome, 107 feet in diameter, that rises above the central nave. Procopius too pays a tribute to the spiritual atmosphere of the church, an atmosphere that neither time nor change of fortune has been able to efface.

St Sophia was not the first church of that name in Con-stantinople. It had two predecessors, the first built by Con-stantine II, son of Constantine the Great, and the second by Theodosius the Younger. Work on Justinian's basilica began in 532, and went forward with such expedition that on 26th December 537 the great church was complete. Twenty-one years later, after the dome had collapsed as the result of an earthquake, repair work had to be put in hand, but this was completed by Christmas Eve 563 when the church was reopened. Since then, despite some further rebuilding (mostly visible on the exterior as additional buttressing) and changes to

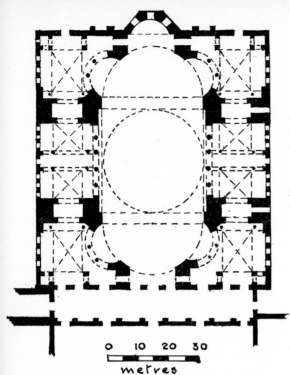

the eastern end of the church in conformity with Moslem principles of orientation, St Sophia has remained substantially intact.

Plate 80   Seen from the outside, St Sophia is not specially impressive,
since to the Byzantine architect it was the interior space and its
organization that was of prime importance. Nor do the four
Turkish minarets improve its appearance, though as Cecil
Stewart has said, they help to emphasize the vast scale of the
church. Originally there would have been a fine view of the
western façade from the colonnaded courtyard, but this has
long since disappeared, apart from the three huge doorways in
its eastern side which give access to the outer porch, or *exonar-
thex*, and so into the *narthex* itself. A gallery above the cross-
vaulted roof of the *narthex* communicates at either end with the
women's galleries above the side aisles, while at ground level
nine doors in the eastern wall of the *narthex* open into the church

Plate 81   itself. Here, over the central square of the nave, a dome rises from spherical triangular pendentives that fill the space between four arches supported on massive piers. To the north and south, the arches are closed by solid walls, supported on arcades in two tiers, of which the lower one of four large columns gives access to the side aisles, while the upper, of six smaller columns, opens into the women's galleries. Both ends of the nave terminate in a semi-dome of the full height and width of the eastern and western arches, and since the central dome is not raised on a drum, the entire nave has the appearance of being roofed over by an elliptical vault. Each semi-dome in its turn is buttressed on either side by a deep *exedra* with two columns at ground- and six at gallery-level. At the eastern end, the apsidal sanctuary performs the function of yet another niche abutment to the semi-dome. However, no bald description such as this can give an adequate idea of the splendour of the interior, adorned with the rarest marbles and precious metals, which Paul the Silentiary celebrated in the panegyric which he composed in hexameters to mark the reopening of St Sophia in 563. The gold and silver have long since disappeared, but the marbles—porphyry, *verde antico*, white Proconnesan and Phrygian pink—still remain to confirm the poet's account. No description either can re-create the soaring quality of the dome which, like the Parthenon at Athens, seems to have alighted only momentarily; nor the immensity of the interior, unbroken from the *narthex* end of the western hemicycle to the eastern apse. All must be seen to be fully appreciated.

The plan of the domed basilica was perfected once and for all in the creation of Anthemius and Isidorus and, as it was never later imitated, St Sophia remains unique, as well as being the supreme achievement of Byzantine architecture. But though the church is generally recognized as a work of original genius, the source, or sources of inspiration for its plan has given rise to hot dispute. Very briefly, extreme points of view are held, on the one hand by those who, like Strzygowski, believe that

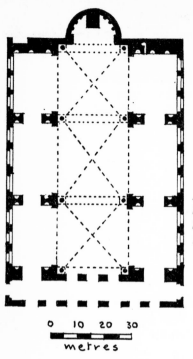

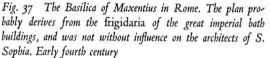

Fig. 37   The Basilica of Maxentius in Rome. The plan pro-
bably derives from the frigidaria of the great imperial bath
buildings, and was not without influence on the architects of S.
Sophia. Early fourth century

St Sophia is for all practical purposes an import into Constantinople of the Armenian domed quatrefoil church with an
ambulatory, and on the other by scholars like Zaloziecky, who
seek to explain the plan solely in terms of the concrete vaulted
architecture of Rome under the late Empire. Of the two
claims, the first is extravagant, while the second needs too much
special pleading and manipulation of possibilities to be
acceptable either. The Armenian thesis, even with its grudging
admission that the galleries over the side aisles are a Hellenistic
feature, is untenable, since St Sophia is, first and foremost, a
basilical church. Even without its western *atrium*, the importance
of the longitudinal axis is stressed by the continuous vista
through the nave to the sanctuary. In this special case, Zaloziecky's suggestion that the basic structure of St Sophia is
Fig. 37   directly derived from the Basilica of Maxentius at Rome
is most valuable, and is accepted by Ward-Perkins who is

otherwise critical of Zaloziecky's partisan approach. However, to admit that the layout of the great church when reduced to its simplest terms closely follows that of the Basilica of Maxentius, and that the arrangements made in both to counter the lateral thrust of the roof are substantially the same, is not also to be committed to the view that the unusual features of St Sophia, the central dome over a square bay, its huge semi-domed abutments and the use of columnar *exedrae* are all explicable in terms of earlier architectural experiments in Rome. The open *exedra* at either end of a rectangular hall does indeed occur in both buildings, and Ward-Perkins apparently follows Zaloziecky in believing that there is no need to look farther afield for prototypes of this feature in St Sophia. Nevertheless, in seventh-century Armenia such *exedrae* were used to buttress a dome, while those in the Roman bath-buildings were not. It is perilous to argue from the unknown, and the balance of probability inclines to the 'Roman' view, but the possible influence of some early version of the Armenian domed quatrefoil church cannot be entirely excluded. There is nothing very startling in the use of columnar *exedrae* in St Sophia, for they were already known in Constantinople in the church of SS. Sergius and Bacchus. Their possible origin in the Eastern Mediterranean has already been touched upon.

The problems connected with the raising of a dome over a square bay have been discussed in an earlier chapter. In St Sophia it was solved by means of spherical triangular pendentives, but these had never before been used in a building of such size. Indeed, the earliest known pendentives, in the tombs on the Via Nomentana near Rome and in the sanctuary of Menas near Alexandria, are of such modest proportions that it seems unlikely, in the absence of further evidence, that Anthemius and Isidorus were indebted to experimental work of this type. Mention of Armenian influence is again purely speculative, and Syria provides no securely dated examples on a monumental scale. In fact, the huge pendentives used in St Sophia represent a new departure in the principles of domical construction, and as such they were apparently recognized by Paul the Silentiary in his magnificent description of them:

Plate 81

'For where the arches necessarily bend away from each other, and would otherwise have shown daylight, a curved wall, like a triangle, inclines forward to touch the edge of the arches on either side; and the four triangles, spread gradually outwards, until they unite over the top of each arch.'

So far no mention has been made of the influence of the earlier domed basilicas of Asia Minor on the plan of St Sophia.

Fig. 30

In architectural detail, this may have been negligible, for the monastery-church at Alahan, for example, is basically an orthodox Hellenistic basilica, which St Sophia is certainly not. Furthermore, despite the squinch arches at the angles of the tower, the Isaurian church was not domed. However, architectural detail is in this instance less important than the principle of combining in one building the longitudinal emphasis required of a basilical church with the vertical emphasis proper to a centralized *martyrium*. It is in this respect then that the architects of Asia Minor in the fifth century played a not inconsiderable role in formulating the idea that inspired the basic plan of St Sophia.

Outside architecture, in the field of ivory carving and metal work, of manuscript illustration and textile production, the Justinianic age brought with it a fresh brilliance. In Constantinople and Ravenna, the style usually represented a blend of elements drawn from a number of sources—though one of these might well predominate—while in the East, many important areas, like Asia Minor, Syria and Egypt, stood firm

Plate 64

by their old traditions. Thus, the supposed provenance of the famous ivory throne of Maximian, Bishop of Ravenna between 546 and *c*. 556, has led to great controversy, since the style of the various panels which were finally assembled by one master craftsman are anything but uniform. In fact, at least four hands are recognizable in the carving. On the front, the figures of St John the Baptist and the four Evangelists against an arcaded background suggest an artist familiar with the Sidamara group of sarcophagi, though the influence of Antiochene Hellenism is strong in the beardless Evangelist representing St John. On both sides of the backrest, panels illustrating New Testament scenes are carved in much lower relief. The treatment is reminiscent of the picturesque style earlier associated with Alexandrian art, while a nice classical touch is the Jordan depicted as a swimming river-god in the scene of Our Lord's Baptism. The panels on both sides of the throne illustrate the life of Joseph in a very individual style, in which the Eastern element specially predominates. Their subject matter has often been taken to denote an Egyptian origin, though there is little in the treatment to connect it with contemporary Coptic art, which is generally much more harsh. The ultimate source might well have been farther East, for many of the figures and their clothing have an almost Greco-Iranian appearance. The last of the artists concerned supplied the decorative ivory bands which separate the panels or act as borders to them. These are carved with deep-cut scroll work of a type generally associated with Syria, and which appears a century earlier on the jambs and lintel block of the south door Plates 27, 29 of the monastery-church at Alahan in Isauria. Primarily on the strength of the New Testament and Joseph panels, the throne has often been attributed to Alexandria, and of course it may be argued that the others, probably representing the styles of Anatolia and Antioch, may well have been carved by native craftsmen living and working in Egypt. By the same token, Antioch is surely no more and no less likely as the centre where the panels were first collected together, particularly as the scroll work was the last to be done before the throne was finally assembled. On balance, however, it is much more likely that the throne was commissioned and made in Constantinople, the Paris of the ancient world, where artists and craftsmen from all over the civilized world could be found working together in the traditional styles to which they were accustomed.

Even if the throne of Maximian was actually manufactured in Constantinople—and it is unlikely that such a hypothesis can ever be proved—it would still not be truly representative of Byzantine art in the First Golden Age. Where silver work is concerned, however, the ground is firmer, since many pieces bear control marks which sometimes provide evidence of origin as well as of date. One such is the large silver-gilt dish used by Paternus, Bishop of Tomi on the Black Sea in the decade before Justinian's accession. Its decoration, in repoussé, is of the simplest, and consists of a central chi-rho flanked by the letters Alpha and Omega, with an inhabited vine scroll round the rim. This is the language of symbolism, and it is used also in another perhaps slightly earlier dish (in Istanbul) this time without a control stamp. Here the centre is filled by a seated female figure with two monkeys at her feet and a parrot and a guinea-fowl in the field. She personifies India, and despite some Oriental features, is clearly in the direct line of classical tradition. This Neo-Attic style seems to have been very popular in Constantinople at this time, and in provincial centres where the influence of the capital was strong. A silver bowl, found at Kyrenia in Cyprus and now in the British Museum, with the bust of St Sergius or St Bacchus in a central medallion, proves the survival of the classical tradition in the early seventh century, while in the contemporary silver-gilt Concesti amphora, now in the Hermitage Museum in Leningrad, the subject matter is drawn direct from pagan mythology. In some fields of art, Constantinople, though open to influences from all the known world, was still the natural guardian of the classical heritage.

Fig. 38   Two fifth-century Christian symbols from opposite ends of the Christian world: (a) on a sarcophagus in the cemetery at Balabolu (Adrassos?) in Isauria; (b) on a tombstone from southern Galloway in Scotland

Manuscript illustrations tend, on the other hand, rather to reflect the Oriental side of Byzantine artistic achievement. The picturesque Alexandrian element is prominent in many of the episodes depicted in the Vienna Genesis, which probably belongs to the late fifth century and was painted by several different artists. Such a scene as the one of Jacob with his flocks against a landscape background may well derive from the original Septuagint illustrations. More homogeneous are the illustrations of the Rossano Codex, which seems to have been illuminated in either Asia Minor or Constantinople in the middle of the sixth century. The squat, heavy headed figures, with their large gestures and formalized drapery are in the Ana-tolian tradition, but the scenes themselves have a maturity and sense of arrangement that suggests that they were painted by an artist resident in the capital. Moreover, the iconography is fully developed, to the extent that such scenes as the Communion of the Apostles and the Raising of Lazarus in the Codex remain current for centuries, as can be seen in the wall paintings of the same events in the churches of Bogoroditsa Leviska at Prizren in Serbia and of the Pantanassa at Mistra in the fourteenth and fifteenth centuries respectively. Of all the miniatures, the most striking represents the Entry of Christ into Jerusalem on the first Palm Sunday. Here is a picture in which the sense of occasion is fully realized in the majestic progress of

Plate 79

Fig. 39   Some importa

Scale in Miles

0   500

Sirmium

DACIA

THRACE

MACEDONIA

Salonika

Dodona

Athens

Corinth

Adamaklissi

Sardica

BLACK SEA

Constantinople

Chalcedon

Nicomedia

Nicaea

PONTUS

Bagaran

Caesarea in Cappadocia

Amida

Nisibis

Smyrna

Ephesus

Hieropolis

Pepuza

Edessa

Dura Europos

Aphrodisias

Sagalassus

Binbirkilise

Cremna

Antioch

Kirkbizze

SEE INSET

CRETE

CYPRUS

SEA

SEA

Ezra

Garizim

Bosra

Salah

Um-al-Jemal

Jerusalem

Bethlehem

Alexandria

EGYPT

RED SEA

~H.A.S~

Christ, the bearded, awe-inspiring figure of East Christian art; some of the people of Jerusalem welcome Him by spreading their garments in His path, while others stand with palm fronds raised high above their heads; the children, eager to join in the excitement, come rushing out of the city gates. Beside this gorgeous scene, with its rich array of bright colours and gold against the purple background of the vellum, the sarco-

Plate 40

phagus relief of the same subject in the Terme Museum appears as a pale reflexion.

In works such as these are mirrored the architectural and artistic achievement of Byzantium's first Golden Age; and because Christianity was the inspiration of Byzantine civiliza-tion, the period of Justinian is also, materially speaking at least, the first Golden Age of Christendom. But the story of Byzantium is not the whole story. Outside the Emperor's domains in the East, Christianity had already spread into Mesopotamia and Persia, and from Edessa and Nisibis Nesto-rian missionaries penetrated Turkestan, and even China itself.

Fig. 38

In the west, St Ninian had spread the faith in the Galloway area, where rough grave-stones with the chi-rho symbol are as evocative as the most splendid monument of New Rome; St Patrick, consecrated bishop by St Martin of Tours himself, had carried out his mass conversions of the Irish; and before the end of the sixth century, St Augustine, as emissary of Pope Gregory the Great, had established his mission to the English. Of all that was won in the East, the larger part, and Byzantium itself, has now been lost. The tide of Christianity ebbs and flows, no less now than it has always done, from its beginnings as a 'baneful superstition' in first-century Rome; but, like the tide, its progress is inexorable.

> *For while the tired waves, vainly breaking,*
> *Seem here no painful inch to gain,*
> *Far back, through creeks and inlets making,*
> *Comes silent, flooding in, the main.*

Select Bibliography

ATTWATER T., *The Christian Churches of the East*, 2 vol., Milwaukee, 1946–7.

BAYNES, N., and MOSS, H., *Byzantium*, Oxford, 1948.

BRITISH MUSEUM, *The Codex Sinaiticus and the Codex Alexandrinus*, London, 1955.

CALDER, W. M., 'Early Christian Epitaphs from Phrygia', *Anatolian Studies*, V, 1955.

Cambridge Ancient History, X, XI, and XII, Cambridge, 1934 and 1939.

Cambridge Mediaeval History, I, Cambridge, 1936.

CARRINGTON, P., *The Early Christian Church*, 2 vol., Cambridge, 1957.

CLAPHAM, A. W., *English Romanesque Architecture before the Conquest*, Oxford, 1936.

CREHAN, J. H., *Athenagoras*, London, 1956.

CROWFOOT, J. W., 'Early Churches in Palestine', *The Schweich Lectures of the British Academy*, 1937.

CUMONT, F., *The Oriental Religions in Roman Paganism*, New York, 1956.

CURLE, A. O., *The Treasure of Traprain*, Glasgow, 1923.

DALTON, O. M., *Byzantine Art and Archaeology*, Oxford, 1911.

DALTON, O. M., *East Christian Art*, Oxford, 1925.

DAVIES, G., *The Origin and Development of Early Christian Architecture*, London, 1952.

DE PAOR, M. and L., *Early Christian Ireland*, London, 1958.

DIEHL, C., *History of the Byzantine Empire*, Princeton, 1925.

DIX, G., *The Shape of the Liturgy*, London, 1945.

DYGGVE, E., *History of Salonikan Christianity*, Oslo, 1951.

FORSYTH, G. H., 'Archaeological Notes on a Trip through Cilicia', *Dumbarton Oaks Papers*, XI, 1957.

FORTESCUE, A., *A Study of the Roman Liturgy*, London, 1930.

GOUGH, M. R. E., 'Anazarbus', *Anatolian Studies*, II, 1952.

GOUGH, M. R. E., 'A Temple and Church at Ayaş', *ibid.*, IV, 1954.

GOUGH, M. R. E., 'Some Recent Finds at Alahan', *ibid.*, V, 1955.

GOUGH, M. R. E., 'A Fifth Century Silver Reliquary from Isauria', *Byzantinoslavica*, XIX (2), 1958.

HAMILTON, J. A., *Byzantine Architecture and Decoration*, London, 1956.

HARNACK, A., *The Expansion of Christianity in the First Three Centuries*, 2 vol., London, 1904–5.

KIRSCHBAUM, E., *The Tomb of St Peter and St Paul*, London, 1959.

KITZINGER, E., *Early Mediaeval Art in the British Museum*, London, 1955.

KLEIST, J. A., *The Epistles of St Clement of Rome and St Ignatius of Antioch*, Westminster, Maryland, 1946.

KLEIST, J. A., *St Polycarp, Bishop of Smyrna*, Cork, 1948.

LAWRENCE, M., 'City-Gate Sarcophagi', *Art Bulletin*, 1927.

LAWRENCE, M., 'Columnar Sarcophagi in the Latin West', *ibid.*, 1932.

LAWRENCE, M., 'The Sarcophagi of Ravenna', *ibid.*, 1945.

LEVI, D., *Antioch Mosaic Pavements*, 2 vol., Princeton, 1947.

MAIURI, A., *Roman Painting*, London, 1953.

MARROU, M., *St Augustine*, London, 1957.

MARTINDALE, C. C., *The Religion of Imperial Rome*, London, 1956.

MEATES, G. W., *Lullingstone Roman Villa*, London, 1955.

MOREY, C. R., 'The Origin of the Asiatic Sidamara Sarcophagi', *American Journal of Archaeology*, XXXVI, 1922.

MOREY, C. R., 'The Chronology of the Asiatic Sarcophagi', *ibid.*, XXXVII, 1923.

MOREY, C. R., *Early Christian Art*, 1935.

RAMSAY, W., *Cities and Bishoprics of Phrygia*, 2 vol., Oxford, 1895–7.

RAMSAY, W., and BELL, G., *The Thousand and One Churches*, London, 1909.

RICE, D. TALBOT, *Byzantine Art*, London, 1954.

RICE, D. TALBOT, *The Beginnings of Christian Art*, London, 1957.

RICE, D. TALBOT, *The Art of Byzantium*, London, 1959.

ROBERTSON, D. S., *Greek and Roman Architecture*, Cambridge, 1945.

ROSTOVTZEFF, M. I., *Excavations at Dura Europos, Preliminary Report on Fifth Season of Work*, Oxford, 1934.

SRAWLEY, J. H., *The Early History of the Liturgy*, Cambridge, 1947.

STEWART, C., *Simpson's History of Architectural Development*, II, London, 1954.

STRZYGOWSKI, J., *The Origins of Christian Church Art*, Oxford, 1923.

SWIFT, E. H., *Hagia Sophia*, New York, 1940.
SWIFT, E. H., *Roman Sources of Christian Art*, New York, 1951.
TOYNBEE, J. M. C., 'The Shrine of St Peter and its Setting', *Journal of Roman Studies*, XLIII, 1953.
TOYNBEE, J. M. C., and WARD-PERKINS, J. B., *The Shrine of St Peter and the Vatican Excavations*, London, 1956.
VAN DE MEER, F., and MOHRMANN, C., *Atlas of the Early Christian World*, London, 1959.
VASILIEV, A. A., *History of the Byzantine Empire*, London, 1952.
VOLBACH, F. W., and HIRMER, M., *Early Christian Art*, London, 1961.
WALTERS ART GALLERY, *Early Christian and Byzantine Art*, Baltimore, 1947.
WAND, J. W. C., *A History of the Early Church*, London, 1952.
WARD-PERKINS, J. B., 'The Italian Element in Late Roman and Early Mediaeval Architecture', *Proceedings of the British Academy*, XXXIII, 1947.
WARD-PERKINS, J. B., 'The Shrine of St Menas in the Maryut', *Papers of the British School at Rome*, XVII, 1949.
WARD-PERKINS, J. B., 'Constantine and the Christian Basilica', *ibid.*, XXII, 1954.

FRENCH

BENOIT, F., *Sarcophages paléochrétiens d'Arles et de Marseille*, Paris, 1954.
BREHIER, L., *La Sculpture et les Arts mineurs byzantins*, Paris, 1936.
CUMONT, F., *Les Mystères de Mithra*, Paris, 1902.
DIEHL, C., *Manuel d'Art byzantin*, 2 vol., Paris, 1925–6.
GRABAR, A., *Martyrium; Recherches sur les Cultes des Reliques et l'Art chrétien antique*, 3 vol., Paris, 1943–6.
LASSUS, J., *Sanctuaires chrétiens de Syrie*, Paris, 1947.
LAURENT, M., *L'Art chrétien des Origines à Justinien*, Brussels, 1956.
PIERCE, H., and TYLER, R., *L'Art byzantin*, 2 vol., Paris, 1932–4.
STRZYGOWSKI, J., *L'ancien Art chrétien de Syrie*, Paris, 1936.
WEIDLE, W., *Mosaiques paléochrétiennes et byzantines*, Milan, 1954.

GERMAN

GERKE, F., 'Ideengeschichte der altchristlichen Kunst', *Zeitschrift für Kirchengeschichte*, LVII, 1940.

GERKE, F., 'Die christliche Sarkophage der vorkonstantinischen Zeit', *Studien zur spätantike Kunstgeschichte*, II, 1933.

GUYER, S., 'Die Bedeutung der Christlichen Baukunst des innere Kleinasiens für die allgemeine Kunstgeschichte', *Byzantinische Zeitschrift*, XXXIII, 1933.

HERZFELD, E., and GUYER, S., *Monumenta Asiae Minoris Antiqua*, II, Manchester, 1928.

KEIL, J., and WILHELM, A., *Monumenta Asiae Minoris Antiqua*, III, Manchester, 1931.

KOLLWITZ, J., *Die Lipsanothek von Brescia*, Berlin, 1933.

STRZYGOWSKI, J., *Kleinasien, ein Neuland der Kunstgeschichte*, Leipzig, 1903.

STRZYGOWSKI, J., *Die Baukunst der Armenier und Europa*, Leipzig, 1918.

WILPERT, G., *Die Malereien der Katakomben Roms*, 2 vol., Friburg im Breisgau, 1903.

ZALOZIECKY, W. R., *Die Sophienkirche in Konstantinopel und ihre Stellung in der Abendlandischen Architektur*, Rome, 1936.

ITALIAN

BOVINI, G., *Mosaici di Ravenna*, Milan, 1956.

BOVINI, G., *Chiese di Ravenna*, Novara, 1957.

BOVINI, G., *La Vita di Cristo nei Mosaici di S. Apollinare Nuovo di Ravenna*, Ravenna, 1959.

BOVINI, G., and OTTOLENGHI, L., *Catalogo della Mostra degli Avori dell'alto Medioevo*, Ravenna, 1956.

CREMA, L., 'L'Architettura di S. Vitale', *Arte Cristiana*, 1947.

MAZZOTTI, M., *La Basilica di S. Apollinare in Classe*, Vatican, 1954.

MAZZOTTI, M., 'Appunti per la Storia della Cattedra eburnea di Ravenna', *Studi Romagnoli*, V, 1956.

VERZONE, P., *L'Architettura religiosa dell'alto Medioevo nell'Italia settentrionale*, Milan, 1942.

SPANISH

PIDAL, R. MENENDEZ, *Historia de España*, II, Madrid, 1939–59.

Sources of Illustrations

Acknowledgements are made to the following individuals and institutions for photographs used in the plates—Anderson: 16, 35, 38, 39, 54, 66; Alinari: 17, 21, 53, 59, 60, 62, 65, 67, 68; Mr Michael Ballance: 7, 22, 27, 29; the Trustees of the British Museum, London: 1, 52, 55–8, 61; Dr Ludwig Budde: 70, 71; National Museum of Antiquities, Edinburgh: 50, 51; Dr Max Hirmer: 9–12, 14, 15, 31–4, 43, 45, 63, 64, 72–8, 80, 81; Mr Islay de C. Lyons: 3, 5, 6, 8, 13, 20, 30, 36, 37, 40; John Rylands Library, Manchester: 4; Thames and Hudson Photo Archive: 2, 24, 25, 41, 79.

With the exception of the map (Fig. 39), which was drawn by Mr H. A. Shelley, all the drawings and plans were made for this volume by my wife. (Fig. 1 is after E. Dyggve; Fig. 3 after G. U. S. Corbett; Figs. 4, 5 after J. M. C. Toynbee and J. B. WardPerkins; Figs. 7, 18, 26 after D. S. Robertson; Figs. 16, 19, 20, 35, 37 after J. B. WardPerkins; Figs. 21, 23, 27, 28, 29, 36 after Cecil Stewart; Fig. 22 after W. M. Ramsay and Gertrude Bell; Fig. 24 after M. Laurent; Fig. 25 after J. Strzygowski.)

ΕΝΑΡΧΗΗΝΟΛΟΓ
ΚΑΙΟΛΟΓΟΣΗΝ
ΠΡΟΣΤΟΝΘΝΚΑΙ
ΘΣΗΝΟΛΟΓΟΣΟΥ
ΤΟΣΗΝΕΝΑΡΧΗ
ΠΡΟΣΤΟΝΘΝΠΑ
ΤΑΛΙΑΥΤΟΥΓΕΝ
ΤΟΚΑΙΧΩΡΙΣΑΥΤ
ΕΓΕΝΕΤΟΟΥΔΕΝ
ΟΓΕΓΟΝΕΝΕΝΑΥ
ΤΩΖΩΗΕΣΤΙΝ
ΚΑΙΗΖΩΗΗΝΤ
ΦΩΣΤΩΝΑΝΘΡ
ΠΩΝΚΑΙΤΟΦΩ
ΕΝΤΗΣΚΟΤΙΑΦΑ
ΝΕΙΚΑΙΗΣΚΟΤΙ
ΑΑΥΤΟΟΥΚΑΤΕ
ΛΑΒΕΝ

ΕΓΕΝΕΤΟΑΝΘΡΩ
ΠΟΣΑΠΕΣΤΑΛΜ
ΝΟΣΠΑΡΑΘΥ
ΝΟΜΑΑΥΤΩΙΩ
ΑΝΝΗΣΟΥΤΟΣ
ΗΛΘΕΝΕΙΣΜΑΡΤ
ΡΙΑΝΙΝΑΜΑΡΤΥ
ΡΗΣΗΠΕΡΙΤΟΥΦ
ΤΟΣΙΝΑΠΑΝΤΕ
ΠΙΣΤΕΥΣΩΣΙΝ
ΑΥΤΟΥΟΥΚΗΝΕΚΙ
ΝΟΣΤΟΦΩΣΑΛ
ΛΙΝΑΜΑΡΤΥΡΗ
ΠΕΡΙΤΟΥΦΩΤΟ
ΗΝΤΟΦΩΣΤΟΑ
ΛΗΘΕΙΝΟΝΟ
ΤΙΖΕΙΠΑΝΤΑΑ
ΘΡΩΠΟΝΕΡΧΟ
ΜΕΝΟΝΕΙΣΤΟΝ
ΚΟΣΜΟΝΕΝΤΩ
ΚΟΣΜΩΗΝΚΑΙ
ΟΚΟΣΜΟΣΔΙΑΥ
ΤΟΝΕΓΕΝΕΤΟΚΑΙ
ΟΚΟΣΜΟΣΑΥΤΟ
ΟΥΚΕ ΕΙΣΤΑ
ΤΑΙΔΙΑΗΛΘΕΝΚΑΙ
ΟΙΙΔΙΟΙΑΥΤΟΝ
ΟΥΠΑΡΕΛΑΒΟΝ
ΟΣΟΙΔΕΕΛΑΒΟΝ
ΑΥΤΟΝΕΔΩΚΕΝ

ΑΥΤΟΙΣΕΞΟΥΣΙΑΝ
ΤΕΚΝΑΘΥΓΕΝΕ
ΤΟΙΣΠΙΣΤΕΥΟΥΣΙ
ΕΙΣΤΟΟΝΟΜΑΑΥΤ
ΟΙΟΥΚΕΞΑΙΜΑΤΩ
ΟΥΔΕΕΚΘΕΛΗΜΑ
ΤΟΣΣΑΡΚΟΣΟΥΔΕ
ΘΕΛΗΜΑΤΟΣΑΝΔΡ
ΑΛΛΕΚΘΥΕΓΕΝΝΗ
ΘΗΣΑΝΚΑΙΟΛΟΓ
ΣΑΡΞΕΓΕΝΕΤΟΚΑΙ
ΕΣΚΗΝΩΣΕΝΕΝΗ
ΜΙΝΚΑΙΕΘΕΑΣΑ
ΜΕΘΑΤΗΝΔΟΞΑ
ΑΥΤΟΥΔΟΞΑΝΩΣ
ΜΟΝΟΓΕΝΟΥΣΠΑ
ΡΑΠΑΤΡΟΣΠΛΗΡΗ
ΧΑΡΙΤΟΣΚΑΙΑΛΗΙΑ
ΙΩΑΝΝΗΣΜΑΡΤΥ
ΠΕΡΙΑΥΤΟΥΚΑΙΚ
ΕΚΡΑΓΕΝΟΥΤΟΣΗΝ
ΟΟΠΙΣΩΜΟΥΕΡ
ΧΟΜΕΝΟΣΟΣΕΜ
ΠΡΟΣΘΕΝΜΟΥΓ
ΓΟΝΕΝΟΤΙΠΡΩ
ΜΟΥΗΝΟΤΙΕΚΤ
ΠΛΗΡΩΜΑΤΟΣΑΥ
ΤΟΥΗΜΕΙΣΠΑΝΤ
ΕΛΑΒΟΜΕΝΚΑΙΧΑ
ΡΙΝΑΝΤΙΧΑΡΙΤΟΣ
ΟΤΙΟΝΟΜΟΣΔΙΑ
ΜΩΥΣΕΩΣΕΔΟΘ
ΗΧΑΡΙΣΚΑΙΗΑΛΗ
ΑΔΙΑΙΥΕΓΕΝΕΤΟ
ΘΝΟΥΔΕΙΣΕΩΡΑ
ΚΕΝΠΩΠΟΤΕΜ
ΝΟΓΕΝΗΣΘΣΟΕΡ
ΚΟΛΠΟΝΤΟΥΠΑ
ΤΡΟΣΕΚΕΙΝΟΣΕΞΗ
ΓΗΣΑΤΟΚΑΙΑΥΤΗ
ΕΣΤΙΝΗΜΑΡΤΥΡΙ
ΑΤΟΥΙΩΑΝΝΟΥΤ
ΑΠΕΣΤΙΛΑΝΟΙΙΟΥ
ΔΑΙΟΙΕΞΙΕΡΟΣΟΛ
ΜΩΝΙΕΡΙΣΚΑΙΛΑ
ΕΙΤΑΣΙΝΑΕΠΕΡΩ
ΤΗΣΩΣΙΝΑΥΤΟΝ
ΤΙΣΕΙΚΑΙΩΜΟΛΟ

2
3

4

5

6

8   7

11

12

13

14

15

18

19

20

22   23

24   25

26

27

28

29

31

32

33

34

MVNIFICENTIA LEONIS·XIII·P·M·

35

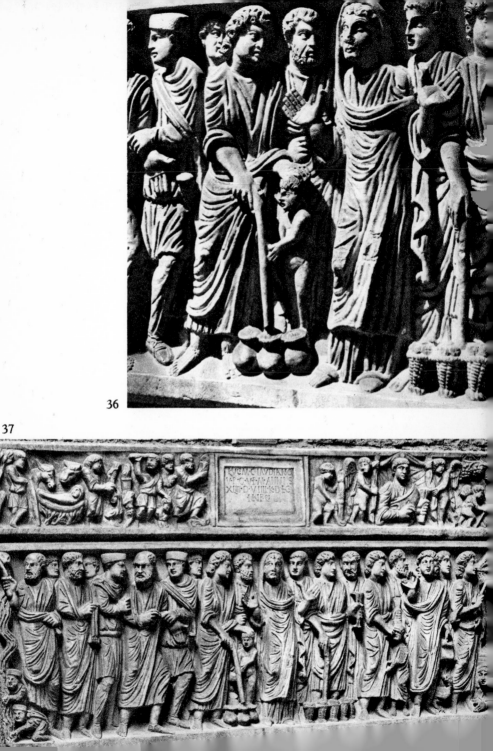

36

37

38

39

40

41

42

43

44

45

46

47

48

49

50

51

52

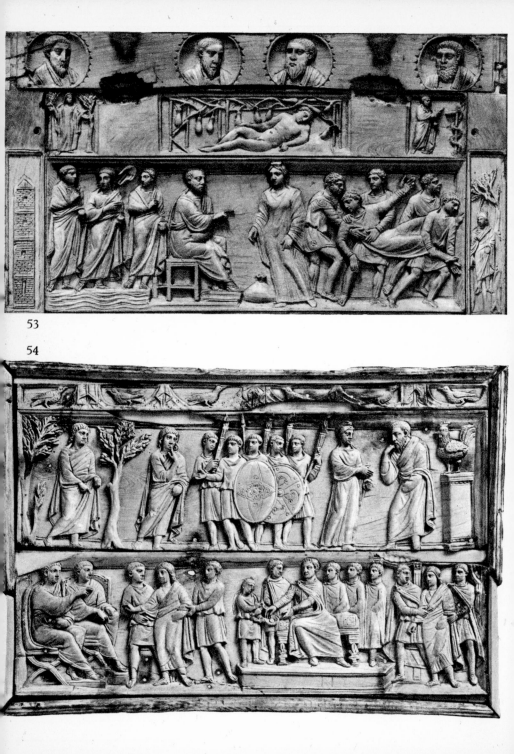

53

54

55

56

57

58

59   60

61

62

63

65

66

67

68

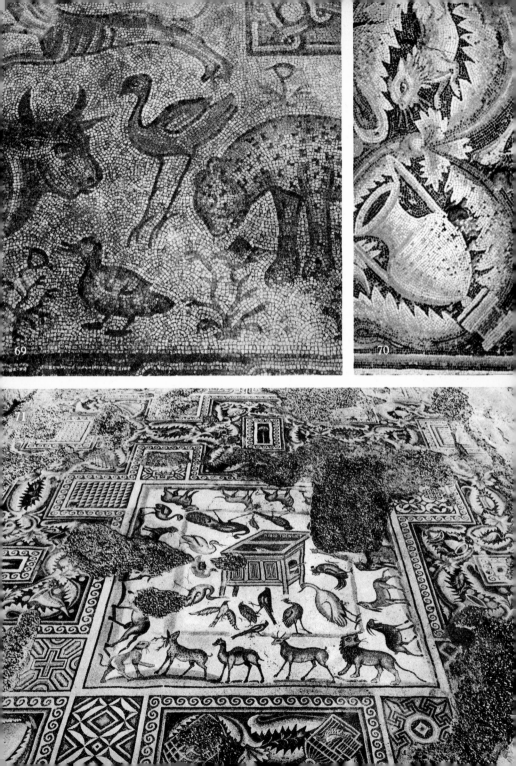

69

70

71

74

75

77

78

Notes on the Plates

1 The beginning of the Gospel of St John in the *Codex Sinaiticus*. In black uncials on vellum. Discovered at the Monastery of St Catherine on Mt Sinai in separate parts, in 1844 and 1859 respectively. Of 390 leaves (covering parts of the Old, and the entire New Testament), all but 43, placed in the University Library at Leipzig in 1844, were acquired in 1867 by the Russian Imperial Government. Purchased for £100,000 in 1933 by the British Museum. Likely provenance, Alexandria or Palestine. First half of the fourth century. London, British Museum.

2 Detail of the Baptistery at Dura Europus on the Euphrates. Left, the covered font with fresco of the Good Shepherd at the west end of the room. Facing, on the north wall, are other frescoes. Above, the Healing of the Paralytic and Christ walking on the Sea; below, the Three Marys at the Sepulchre (here shown as a sarcophagus). The subject of the latter is disputed. *c.* 240. Yale University, Gallery of Fine Arts.

3 The Basilica of Maxentius in Rome. Constructed of brick-faced concrete on a gigantic scale—the vault over the great central hall spanned more than 70 ft—it seems to have derived its plan from the *frigidaria* of Imperial bath-buildings. The side aisles were broken up by transverse walls into three huge vaulted bays with coffered ceilings, but the longitudinal emphasis was partially preserved by doorways connecting the several bays. The building was planned and begun by Maxentius, but completed by Constantine, with some tasteless additions, after 312.

4 Fragmentary papyrus leaf (originally part of a bound book) containing passages from the Passion of Our Lord according to St John. Acquired in Egypt in 1923, it is the earliest known manuscript of the New Testament. Second half of the second century. Manchester, John Rylands Library.

5 Part of a funerary inscription, the so-called Monument of Avircius from Hieropolis in Phrygia. Inscribed in the lifetime of the bishop, it was

discovered by Professor W. M. Ramsay in 1883, and restored by means of a previously known *Life of Avircius* which quoted the epitaph in full. The part here preserved begins: ['He (a Pure Shepherd) sent me] to Rome to see Sovereignty and to look upon a Queen with golden raiment and golden sandals.' Early third century. Rome, Museo Cristiano Lateranense.

6 Sarcophagus fragment from Rome, illustrating a *refrigerium*, or refreshment meal, of bread and wine at a sigma-table. On the right, the Shepherd and the right arm of an *orans*. Third-fourth century. Rome, Museo delle Terme.

7 Sacred carp in the fish-pond in front of the Mosque of Ibrahim Paşa at Urfa (Edessa). A survival of the worship of Atargatis, the Syrian fish-goddess?

8 Panel from top right-hand corner of the sarcophagus of Baebia Hermo-phile, from the Via Tiburtina in Rome. The light-hearted treatment of the subject, a refreshment meal in honour of the dead, is more reminiscent of a 'wake' than of a symbol of the Eucharist. Its association on the sarcophagus with the Shepherd and the Jonah story ensures its Christian significance. Late third century. Rome, Museo delle Terme.

9 Fresco in the Crypts of Lucina in the Catacomb of Callixtus at Rome. The Good Shepherd holding with His left hand a sheep across His shoulders, and a cooking pot with His right. Mid third century.

10 Fresco from the Capella Greca in the Catacomb of Priscilla in Rome. The Three Children in the Fiery Furnace, represented as *orantes*. Early fourth century.

11 Fresco from the Catacomb of Priscilla in Rome. Factual representation of the Last Supper, with Christ in the centre of His Apostles. Fourth century.

12 Fresco from the Catacomb of Callixtus in Rome. The soul in Paradise, represented by an *orans* in a garden. Early fourth century.

13 Marble statue of the Good Shepherd, the favourite theme for Early Christian sculpture in the round. Although purely symbolic, it is treated in a naturalistic manner. Late third or early fourth century. Rome, Museo Cristiano Lateranense.

14 Sarcophagus from the church of S. Maria Antiqua in Rome. In the centre, the deceased represented as a seated philosopher, reading from a *volumen* and flanked by (right) the Good Shepherd and (left) an *orans*. Beyond these figures are (right) the Baptism of Christ and (left) Jonah resting beneath the gourd-tree. Third century B.C.

15 Detail of 14.

16 Fresco of a mother and child (the Virgin and Infant Christ?) from the Roman Catacomb named the Coemeterium Maius. This picture well illustrates the trend towards 'expressionism' derived from the Orient and perhaps Syria in particular, during the post-Constantinian period. Fourth century.

17 The Basilica of S. Maria Maggiore in Rome. Although a basilica was originally built on the site by Pope Liberius (352–6), the present structure, with many additions and alterations, dates to the period of Sixtus III (432–40). The two Ionic colonnades, spanned by architraves, originally continued unbroken as far as the sanctuary; the unsightly arches are a sixteenth-century addition. The mosaics on the triumphal arch and above the architraves date to the Pontificate of Sixtus III.

18, 19 The monastery-church, or so-called domed basilica, at Alahan in Isauria. (18) View from north, showing the central tower and inscribed apse flanked by *pastophoria*. In the distance, the Calycadnus valley. (19) View from the north-west. The row of consoles along the western façade helped support a wooden platform which gave access through two small doors to the galleries above the side aisles. The whole building was roofed with timber, that over the tower probably taking the form of a flat pyramid.

20 Exterior of the church of S. Costanza in Rome. Its original dedication is uncertain, but it was fairly early converted into a christian baptistery

after perhaps serving as the Mausoleum of Constantia, a daughter of Constantine I. The drum of the cupola is directly supported on a ring of double columns united by an arcade, and buttressed by the vault of the encircling ambulatory. Early fourth century.

21 Interior of S. Costanza in Rome. Central ring of columns and outer ambulatory. Many of the original mosaics in the vaulting of the ambula-tory are Dionysiac in theme, while the earliest of the specifically Christian mosaics are apparently of fifth century date.

22 Capital from the monastery-church at Alahan in Isauria. Eagles with spread wings replace the angle volutes normal to the Corinthian order. This baroque tendency is discernible in some of the later capitals (third century) in the colonnaded street at Pompeiopolis in eastern Cilicia.

23 Capital from Hieropolis Castabala (Bodrum) on the Pyramus. This window capital has two unusual features in the peacock between the central volutes, and the two serpents immediately below the egg and dart moulding at the top. Early fifth century.

24 Marble capital from S. Sophia in Constantinople. This fully developed work of the First Golden Age well illustrates the 'coloristic' treatment of the old acanthus decoration, while the vegetable form is almost completely stylized. Sixth century.

25 Marble capital from Constantinople, decorated with four heads whose hair and beards are formed of acanthus foliage. Late fifth or early sixth century. Istanbul, Museum of Antiquities.

26 Arcaded vestibule of a basilica at Canytela (Kanlı Divane) in western Cilicia. The acanthus capitals are of 'orthodox' Corinthian type. A single door gives access to the church proper. Fifth century.

27–29 Architectural sculpture from the *narthex* of the western building and the monastery-church at Alahan in Isauria. Mid fifth century. (27) Jamb and lintel of the south door of the monastery church. The carving of vine scrolls with birds pecking at the grapes is interrupted at the corner by an unfinished, roughed-out portion. Such omissions (possibly intentional) are a feature of this sculptor's work. (28) The Archangel St Michael, carved in relief on the southern jamb of the central door. In his right hand he holds an orb; in his left, a pair of scales for weighing the souls of men. His feet rest on two human busts, both much worn. (29) Cornice block (cornerpiece) carved in high relief with realistic vine scrolls. Between horizontal modillions, crossed fish and formalized partridges (?).

30 Colossal portrait head of Constantine from a marble statue in the Basilica of Maxentius in Rome. The head is remarkable for its blend of the old classical naturalistic tradition with the 'expressionism' of the Orient. The square hole near the left eye and the unworked surface above the hair line suggest that a bronze diadem or wreath was originally fitted. Rome, Museo dei Conservatori. *c.* 312.

31 Relief sculpture on the base of the Obelisk of Theodosius in the Hippodrome at Istanbul. On the south-east side, Theodosius, flanked by his two sons Arcadius and Honorius, stands in the imperial box, wreath in hand, ready to crown a victor in the games. Behind him, and on either side of the imperial party, stand armed guards and senators. Below are spectators and entertainers. *c.* 390.

32 Detail from the freize on the northern façade of the Arch of Constantine in Rome. Magistrates and people listen to an *allocutio* of the Emperor in the Forum, represented by the architectural background. The arch was erected after Constantine's victory over Maxentius at the Milvian Bridge in 312.

33 Marble head, probably of the Emperor Arcadius, found at Bayazıt in Istanbul in 1949. The features of the Emperor, who wears a diadem of pearls, resemble those of the less distinguished head of Valentinian II (?) from Aphrodisias, now in Istanbul. Fourth–fifth century. Istanbul, Museum of Antiquities.

34 Marble bust of an Evangelist (?) from Istanbul. Fifth century. Istanbul, Museum of Antiquities.

35 Marble sarcophagus found in the Via Salaria in Rome. The decoration is entirely symbolic. In the centre, the Good Shepherd with His flock; at the ends, a draped male and female figure, each one holding a *volumen* and representing followers of Christ's true philosophy. To the left of the Good Shepherd, an *orans* figure symbolizes the soul of the deceased in Paradise. End of third century. Rome, Museo Cristiano Lateranense.

36, 37 Sarcophagus of Claudianus from the Via della Lungara in Rome. Fourth century. Rome, Museo delle Terme. (36) Detail of 37. (37) The lid shows the Nativity, the Sacrifice of Isaac, Moses receiving the Tables of the Law on Sinai; funerary inscription; Claudianus and *Amores* engaged with the harvest and vintage. The main frieze shows the symbolic baptism of the centurion Cornelius at the water struck from the rock by Moses-Peter, the arrest of St Peter, the miracle of Cana, the Soul in Paradise (symbolized by the praying figure), the Multiplication of the Loaves, the Healing of the Man born blind, the Denial of St Peter, the raising of Lazarus and the Woman with the Issue of Blood.

38 Marble sarcophagus, originally in the Museo Cristiano Lateranense in Rome. Eight elaborate Corinthian columns form a colonnade which breaks up, but does not destroy the continuity of the episodes. Centre: Christ, enthroned above the vault of heaven, hands the New Law to St Peter, while looking towards St Paul, Apostle of the Gentiles; left, the Sacrifice of Isaac; right, Christ before Pilate. Mid-fourth century. Vatican, Grotto of St Peter's.

39 Niched columnar sarcophagus of marble with scenes illustrating the Triumph of the Passion. Second half of the fourth century. Rome, Museo Cristiano Lateranense.

40 Detail of a sarcophagus from La Storta near Rome. Mid fourth century. Rome, Museo delle Terme. Lid: The Denial of St Peter, the Woman with the Issue of Blood, medallion containing the bust of a man carrying a *volumen*; Christ with Adam and Eve. Main Frieze: The first Palm Sunday, the Miracle of Cana, the Healing of the Paralytic

and the Baptism of Cornelius in water struck from the rock by Moses-Peter.

41 Fragmentary marble relief of the Apostles from Bakırköy, possibly representing the *Traditio Legis*. Height, 2 ft 6 in.; width, 5 ft. Late fourth century. Istanbul, Museum of Antiquities.

42 Limestone sarcophagus in the funerary area at Balabolu (Adrassus?) in Isauria. Arcading and episodic treatment of the scene are reminiscent of some fourth-century Christian sarcophagi in Rome and southern Gaul. Late third century (?).

43 Detail of right-hand side of a marble ambo, originally in the church of St George at Salonika. Stylistic affinities with Lydian group of sarcophagi suggest an atelier in Asia Minor. Height, 5 ft 11 in.; width, 2 ft 9 in. Mid fifth century. Istanbul, Museum of Antiquities.

44 Sculptural podium, possibly an altar (?), in the monastery-church at Alahan in Isauria. On a smaller scale, many features of the ambo from Salonika (Pl. 43) are repeated, particularly the arrangement of the niches and the detail of the vine and acanthus scroll above them. Height, *c.* 3 ft 4 in. Mid fifth century.

45 Side of a silver, part-gilded reliquary, decorated in *repoussé* with scenes from the Old and New Testaments. North Italian school. Height, 7 in.; width, 8 in. End of the fourth century. Milan, below the high altar of the church of S. Nazaro.

46–48 Silver reliquary, decorated in *repoussé*, from Çırga in Isauria. Height, 2 in.; with lid, 3 in.; width, 4 in.; depth, 1½ in. Second half of the fifth century. Adana Museum. (46) The end, showing a jewelled cross with two beribboned doves on arms. Below, a male and female bust (the donors?) confronting each other. *Agnus Dei* on lid. (47) The front: a central medallion contains Christ Pantocrator flanked by adorants. On either side of medallion, St Conon in *orans* posture. (48) The back: a central medallion contains two saints, a cross and lamb. On either side, a female saint (St Ia or the Virgin?) in *orans* posture and flanked by lions.

49 Detail of a bronze thurible from Dağ Pazarı in northern Isauria. Christ, with halo, raises His right hand in blessing; in His left, He holds a lamp. Height, 4 in.; width, 2 in. Fifth century. Adana Museum.

50, 51 Silver flask, part gilded, from the treasure found on Traprain Law, near Edinburgh. Decorated with Biblical subjects, and probably an altar cruet. Height, 8½ in. Fourth century. Edinburgh National Museum of Antiquities. (50) This side shows the Adoration of the Magi, the earliest known rendering of the subject in metal work. (51) The Fall of Man.

52 Silver casket, part gilded, from a treasure found on the Esquiline Hill in Rome. The front is inscribed 'Secundus and Proiecta, live in Christ'. In the centre, Proiecta, adorned as a bride, sits under an arcade, attended by two female servants. On the lid, Venus on a sea-shell and Tritons. Height, 11 in.; width, 23¾ in. Fourth century. London, British Museum.

53, 54 Cover and one side of an ivory casket, decorated with scenes from the Old and New Testaments. Probably used as a reliquary. School of Milan. Second half of the fourth century. Brescia, Civico Museo dell' Età Cristiana. Height, 10 in.; width, 13 in.; depth, 11 in. (53) Side: above, medallions with the heads of saints; centre, Jonah sleeping beneath the gourd-tree, flanked by Susannah (left) and Jonah destroying the serpent of Babylon (right); below, Christ calls SS. James and John beside the Sea of Galilee (?), the punishment of Ananias and Sapphira, the Suicide of Judas. (54) Cover: above, the Agony in the Garden, the Arrest of Christ, the Denial of St Peter; below, Christ before Annas and Caiaphas, and before Pilate.

55–58 Sides of an ivory pyxis, with scenes of Our Lord's Passion. Probably made in southern Gaul. Height, 2 in.; width, 4 in. Early fifth century. London, British Museum. (55) Pilate washes his hands; Christ carries His cross; St Peter sits in the courtyard of Caiaphas, warming his hands at the brazier, with the maid-servant to whom he denied Our Lord standing close by. In the corner, the cock, symbolizing St Peter's denial. (56) Christ crucified, with Longinus piercing His left side. On His right, the Virgin and St John. On extreme left, Judas Iscariot hanging from a tree, with the bag containing thirty pieces of silver at his feet. (57) Christ with His Apostles after the Resurrection. St Thomas touches the wound in Our Lord's side. (58) Easter morning. In the centre, the open Sepulchre with the two Marys and sleeping soldiers on either side. On the top right-hand panel of the tomb door, Christ raises Lazarus from the dead.

59, 60 Ivory diptych. Height, 12 in.; width, 5½ in. Fourth–fifth century. Florence, Museo Nazionale (Bargello). (59) Scenes from the life of St Paul. (60) Adam with the beasts in the Garden of Eden.

61 Base of vessel in gilt and gold leaf from Rome. A youthful Christ places garlands on the heads of a husband and wife. Inscription reads 'Mayest thou live, sweet soul'. Diameter, 2½ in. Fourth century. London, British Museum.

62 Medallion in glass and gold leaf of a mother with her son and daughter, set into a Byzantine cross. The inscription is possibly a signature, Bunerius the Potter (Glass-maker?). These arresting portraits strongly resemble paintings on mummy-cases at Fayyum in Egypt in the second century, and may well be the work of an Alexandrian craftsman. Fourth century. Brescia, Civico Museo dell' Età Cristiana.

63 Central medallion on a frieze sarcophagus designed for a husband and wife of the aristocratic class. Fourth century. Syracuse, Museo Nazionale.

64 Ivory throne of Maximian, Bishop of Ravenna (546–c. 556). The work consists of a number of panels carved by different hands in varying styles that suggest the influence of Alexandrian, Syrian and Anatolian art. It may, however, have been worked and assembled at Constantinople. Height, 4 ft 11 in.; width, 2 ft 2 in. Ravenna, Museo Arcivescovile.

65, 66 Carved panels from the wooden doors of the church of S. Sabina (432) in Rome. Some of Our Lord's miracles, balanced by suitable incidents in the Life of Moses. Left, from top to bottom: the Raising of Lazarus, the Multiplication of the Loaves and Fishes, and the Miracle at Cana. Right, from top to bottom: God speaking to Moses from the Burning

Bush, Moses distributing Quails and Manna to the Children of Israel, and Moses striking Water from the Rock. (66) Detail: Christ crucified between the two thieves.

67, 68 The Mausoleum of Galla Placidia in Ravenna. The three sarcophagi inside are traditionally those of Galla Placidia, her husband Constantius, and her son Valentinian III. Mid fifth century. (67) The interior, looking eastwards. The mosaics depict, above, an Apostle on either side of the window; below, in the lunette, St Lawrence approaching his gridiron, with an open book case containing the four Gospels. (68) Detail of the Good Shepherd mosaic in the western lunette above the entrance.

69 Detail of a floor mosaic in the 'pattern-book' style from a small church built inside a pagan temple at Ayaş in western Cilicia. No glass *tesserae* were used, and the white background was arranged as a shell pattern. Late fifth century.

70, 71 Details of a floor mosaic from the great church at Mopsuestia (Misis) in the plain of Eastern Cilicia. The main features of this mosaic are scenes from the life of Samson, a picture of Noah's ark surrounded by animals and birds (71), and decorative 'inhabited' acanthus scrolls used as a border motif (70). Fifth century.

72, 73 Mosaics from the nave of S. Apollinare Nuovo in Ravenna. Miracle of the Multiplication of the Loaves and Fishes (72), and the Last Judgment (73).

74 Mosaic of the Palace of Theodoric from S. Apollinare Nuovo at Ravenna. The scene represents either the façade of the building, or by a recognized convention, the interior with all sides visible at once. If the latter, the two lower arcades on either side of the gabled *Palatium* should be thought of as the long sides of the palace. The single curtains knotted in the middle are a charming reminder of a current domestic fashion in the eastern Mediterranean. Work of the Roman School, executed under Theodoric the Goth. Early sixth century.

75 Interior view of the octagonal Baptistery of the Orthodox (sometimes called the Neonian Baptistery) at Ravenna. The glass mosaics are some

of the most brilliant ever executed, especially those encircling the cupola. The baptistery is also decorated with paintings in grisaille, with reliefs of the saints in plaster and marble slabs in contrasting colours and patterns. Second half of fifth century.

76 Part of the dome mosaic from the church of St George at Salonika. Against a fantastic background of sumptuous architecture in gold and turquoise, stand the Saints of the Eastern Church—here SS. Onesiphorus and Porphyrius—with the dates of their feast-days written beside them. First half of the fifth century.

77 Apse mosaic of S. Vitale in Ravenna. In the centre, Our Lord enthroned on the orb of the world and flanked by two angels. On the left, S. Vitalis receives his crown from Christ; on the right, Bishop Ecclesius with a model of his church. *c. 530*

78 Sanctuary mosaic in the church of S. Vitale in Ravenna, showing the Empress Theodora and her retinue entering the Church. 547.

79 Page of an illustrated Gospel-book (Rossano Codex) in parchment, with silver lettering on a purple ground. The scene represents the Entry of Our Lord into Jerusalem on the First Palm Sunday. Mid sixth century. Rossano, Museo dell'Archivescovado.

80 View, from the south-west, of the church of S. Sophia at Istanbul. The present building replaced a basilical church, also dedicated to the Divine Wisdom. Planned by the architects Anthemius of Tralles and Isidorus of Miletus, it was building from February 532 until December 537. Transformed into a mosque by Sultan Mehmet Fatih in 1453, four minarets were added during the sixteenth century, the latter two in 1572 by the famous architect Sinan. Under the Republic it has been designated a Museum (Aya Sofya Müzesi).

81 The interior of the church of S. Sophia in Istanbul, looking to the south-east. The furniture in and near the apse, together with the lamps and suspended roundels are Moslem accretions.

Index

PART II: *Modern References*

PART III: *General*